Fellowship and Service Projects for Preteens

Tween time

volume 2

Abingdon Press

Contents

Fellowship Programs

Plan Ahead to Party On!

Party On! is the tweens' closing celebration. Preview the program now. Set aside some time each week to plan, gather materials for, and recruit helpers for this awesome celebration of the tweens and their fellowship experience. It's also the time to invite the next year's tweens into the group. The session includes games and recipes, which may be used for the party or anytime during the year.

04 05 06 07 08 09 10 11 12 13—10 9 8 7 6 5 4 3 2 1

Contents

Service Projects

About the Writers

Debbie Branker-Harrod is a middle school teacher. In addition to writing for Sunday school, she has also designed curriculum for HyperTV network eschoolonline.

Mark Bushor is an ordained clergyperson currently serving as pastor to Crossroads Church in Cleburne, Texas, where he delights in introducing tweens and teens to the joy of serving others.

Vida Findley has worked for more than twenty years in children's worship, vacation Bible school, and Sunday school. She has also developed arts-in-education curricula for three to eighteen year olds. She attends Hobson United Methodist Church, Nashville, Tennessee.

Leigh L. Gregg oversees and participates in ministry with tweens (and other age levels) at Sierra Vista United Methodist Church in San Angelo, Texas. She also serves as pastor at Veribest United Methodist, a small nearby church.

James H. Ritchie, Jr., writes frequently for and about tweens. The developer of *Created by God: About Human Sexuality for Older Girls and Boys,* he teaches this study nationwide.

James Wrede has taken his experience as a Christian educator home, where he now concentrates on infants and preschoolers (specifically, one of each of his own). He currently lives in Belleville, Illinois, until the Air Force tells his wife otherwise.

Fellowship and Service With Tweens

By James H. Ritchie, Jr., Ed.D.

The summer after seventh grade, Aaron was a year too young to take part in the annual youth mission project doing home repair in Appalachia. Agency guidelines indicated that participants were to have completed eighth grade, but an exception was made since Aaron would have a parent along. Thank God for that degree of flexibility and the recognition that when preteen passion presents itself, it needs to be acknowledged and nurtured.

Aaron never missed a training session in the months prior to departure. On site, he graciously weathered the good-natured teasing of the older youth. He worked enthusiastically all week, willingly tackling some of the less-desirable tasks—the ones that involved climbing, crawling, and confronting spiders. He became somewhat of the resident mascot during recreation times and was in the middle of laughter, conversations, and group backrubs during informal fellowship hours.

A few months later, eighth grade confirmand Aaron, declared himself an atheist—not necessarily welcome news to parents, pastors, confirmation coordinators, and mentors. Yet while he wrestled with theological doubts, Aaron never indicated a desire to withdraw from confirmation preparation. In fact, he was quite direct in voicing his eagerness to remain involved in youth fellowship and outreach projects, and his hope for continued acceptance in the church.

Many young persons—and adults as well—speak empty words of commitment simply because it is expected of them, because they figure they deserve some recognition for their efforts, or in order to avoid exposing and defending their doubts. Not Aaron. He saw the confirmation process through to the moment of decision, electing not to profess faith.

Aaron tested the system and found it faithful. While no one has abandoned the hope that one day he will be ready to pledge his allegiance to Christ and the church, the congregation continues to live out the commitment made when Aaron was baptized. His ongoing involvement in youth fellowship and mission ministries, initiated during his middle school years, provides him with a place where he invests himself in good work, where he feels good about the church and himself, and where he is both free and supported as he continues to come to terms with matters of faith.

IT'S ABOUT FITTING IN

Aaron may be more honest and a bit more articulate than others his age, but he is far from unusual. What is unusual about this scenario is the patient embrace of the church. Aaron trusted the church enough to feel safe exposing his questions, confident that he would not be dis-fellowshipped in the process. He had discovered as he tried the church on for size during his preteen years that there was a good fit. Here was a place where he belonged, even in time of uncertainty.

Tweens long to fit in. These entry-level adolescents fall from innocence with the discovery that they do not occupy center stage in the universe. That earth-shaking

realization comes to us all sooner or later. While the seismographic reading differs from person to person, no one escapes the quake. We long to fit in, hoping to find a friend or two whose foundations seem to have stabilized—persons to whom we can attach ourselves for safety. The unspoken theory is this: Still reeling from having been displaced as the center of the universe, I need to be able to point to where my personal universe is centered in order to regain some equilibrium.

Can preteens identify that stability among their peers? With all of them going through the same stage, the likelihood of that happening isn't good. Not that there aren't persons standing ready to suggest that it is. "Stability" and "adult" are understood as synonyms, and that's good. However, think about the commodities rated "adult" that are offered as shortcuts to authentic adulthood—adult movies, adult language, adult fashions, adult beverages, adult situations, and adult humor, to name just a few—that provide escape from stability and responsibility. These are some of the things that tweens claim that everyone's doing, and they want above all else to be included.

A weekly Sunday school and worship experience are not enough to counteract all those pressures. Tweens also benefit from regular fellowship opportunities—ones designed to ensure that young persons have a place where they feel as though they fit in with their peers. Such a place is not defined by dress, status, or pseudo-adult behaviors, but by faith, fun, and freedom to be who you are.

IT'S ABOUT MAKING A DIFFERENCE

As tweens search for alternatives to occupy the center of their personal universes, many explore altruistic options. Some of the impetus for this direction is hormonal. They feel things with greater intensity as they begin the journey of adolescence. If not redirected, they can easily become self-absorbed once again, believing that they are the only ones who have ever experienced the travails of growing up. The preteen years are an ideal time to expose them to the needs of other persons—especially those that, unlike adolescence, won't simply go away with time.

Preteens are smart. They know the difference between actually making a difference and being set up to feel as though they have made a difference. If we want to engage them, we have to provide opportunities for them to do the former. Position them to facilitate change in the lives of others, and you reverse their feelings of powerlessness in the presence of all the change that adolescence imposes on them. Everyone wins! Lives are made better, self-esteem skyrockets, and you have crafted a teachable moment where you can say, "Now this is what it means to be a person of faith!"

Aaron might not be sure about God at the moment, but as he continues to enjoy fellowship with the church's youth and as he exercises his body, mind, and heart in service to others, there will be many opportunities to say, "This is what it means to live a life of faith. This is what we call 'God.' This is how we respond to the call of Jesus Christ."

Tweens at All Times

What are tweens at all times?

Curious. They want to know and, with a little encouragement, are willing to venture out in search of the answers to their questions. Before long, they will wander into the know-it-all phase. Not that they will know it all or even want to, but they won't want anyone else to know that they don't—especially when it comes to grown-up stuff. Soon they will be caught up in adolescence and eager for people to not notice or at least not call attention to their "adolescing."

In transition. Neither child nor adult, neither here nor there. They are unsettled, yet growing in so many ways! They are a wonderful metaphor for the church and for Christians on their way to perfection. Enjoy them!

Fellowship Programs

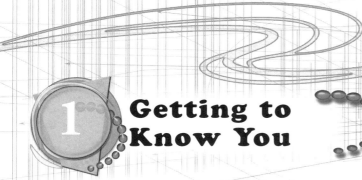

Getting to Know You

LESSON IN A NUTSHELL

Today's tweens are searching for someone they can trust. In "Getting to Know You," tweens will learn more about themselves and one another. They will build a community in which they experience emotional security and trust. Having a group covenant is vital to the development of a safe community.

WHO AM I? (5–8 minutes)

Write well-known names on nametags. These need to be people your tweens will recognize and will be able to ask and answer questions about. For example: your church's pastor, the principal of their school, a local sports hero, or a national celebrity.

As tweens arrive, place a nametag on their back. The tweens are to mingle, asking yes/no questions of one another to determine "Who am I?" When they guess the correct identity, they move their nametag to their front and continue helping others discover "Who am I?"

When all have arrived, say: **It is important to know who we really are. Sometimes we need to ask questions of others and ourselves to find out who we really are. Today we are going to learn more about one another and ourselves.**

PICK A GAME (5–15 minutes)

Choose one or more of the games below to help your tweens learn more about themselves and one another.

Info Bingo: Use the Info Bingo grid from page 10. Fill in the blank spaces with items specific to your location. For example: names of schools, and other locale-specific activities in which your tweens might participate. Make a copy of the grid for each tween. Instruct the tweens to find someone who fits the statement in each box and have that person sign the box. Depending upon the size of your group, you may want to limit the number of times they can have one person sign their grid. When they have a signature in every box, they are to yell, "Info Bingo." At that point, have the tweens sit down and review the info. Review each box, having other tweens who also fit that category raise their hand.

Covenant Community

Special Tips

Tweens need reassurance and support. They expect *you* to be honest with them. Be ready to share yourself with them in order for them to share themselves with you and the rest of the group.

My Best—My Worst: Divide the tweens into groups of three or four. Give each tween one minute to describe his or her best day ever. Call out, "Change!" when one minute is up so that the next tween can have a turn. When all have had a turn, give the tweens one minute to describe their worst day ever. Call out, "Change!" when one minute is up so that the next tween can have a turn. Have the tweens change partners. Repeat the game several times.

Silent Lineup: Instruct the tweens to get into a line in order by categories. This sounds easy; however, they are to do so without talking. Designate one side of the room as the beginning of the line. Have them stand shoulder to shoulder in order of their date of birth. January would come first. Remind them to use the day of their birth as well. When they are in order, have them call out their birthday to see how well they lined up. Think of other "orders" such as by grade, by number of siblings, by number of pets.

WHAT DOES GOD SAY? (10 minutes)

Have one of the tweens read the Scripture lesson from **Genesis 9:8-17.**

Say: **We have spent our time today getting to know one another better. Our Scripture talks about covenant. What is a covenant?** (*A covenant is an agreement between two parties, such as between people or groups of people or between God and people.*)

In order for us to make a covenant with someone, we have to know who that party is and whether or not we can trust each other.

- How did Noah know God? What had been his experience with God before this covenant was offered?
- Why did Noah trust God?

Say: **We are going to make a group covenant outlining how we will relate to one another in this group.**

GROUP COVENANT (5–20 minutes)

Gather the tweens into groups of three or four.

Say: **Our time together should be a time of safety, security, and trust. In order for that to happen, we will need to agree on how to treat one another within this group. In your small groups, come up with three or four statements about how we should treat one another.**

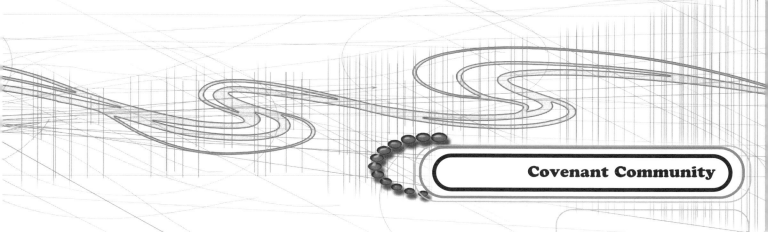

You will want to consider what we do while we are together and what we do while we are apart. You have five minutes to come up with your statements. Then we will report to the entire group and develop a group covenant.

After the small groups have developed their statements, have each group report its statements to the larger group. Ask one of the tweens to write these on large paper or posterboard. Encourage the larger group to work together to develop a list of expectations and covenant statements by which the fellowship group will function.

Be prepared to offer suggestions such as: "what we say here stays here," "respect one another," and a description of appropriate conversation. When the list is complete, have the tweens "sign" the covenant by using poster paint or an ink pad to place their thumbprints on the covenant. Use the litany below to "seal the covenant."

SENDING FORTH (3–6 minutes)

Say: **Today we have learned more about one another and ourselves. We have established a covenant with one another. God sealed the covenant with Noah and his descendants by placing a rainbow in the sky. The sign of our commitment to this covenant is our thumbprints. We will now seal our covenant by joining in prayer together.**

Divide the group into two for the reading.

Group 1: Thank you, God, . . .

Group 2: for our relationship with you.

Group 1: Thank you, God, . . .

Group 2: for our relationships with one another.

Group 1: Help us, God, . . .

Group 2: to treat one another with respect.

Group 1: Help us, God, . . .

Group 2: to keep our covenant with you and one another.

All: With your help, we can keep our covenant. Amen.

When Time Matters

If you have more time, have the tweens use the colors of the rainbow—either to decorate the poster with the covenant printed on it or to do the thumbprint signing.

Depending on the number in the group, if they are attempting to make a rainbow of their thumbprints, they may each need to do multiple thumbprints.

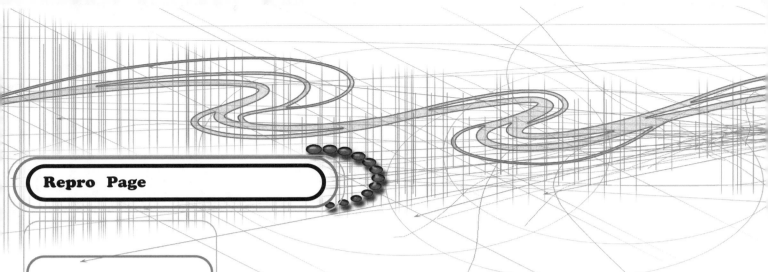

Directions

Move from person to person, asking each one whether he or she fits a description on the grid. When you find someone who fits a description, have him or her sign that square.

As soon as you have all of the squares filled with signatures, call out; "Info Bingo!"

Info Bingo

	Has a brother			
			Has a sister	
Has a dog		Has a pet that is not a dog or cat		
				Plays soccer
	Plays the piano			

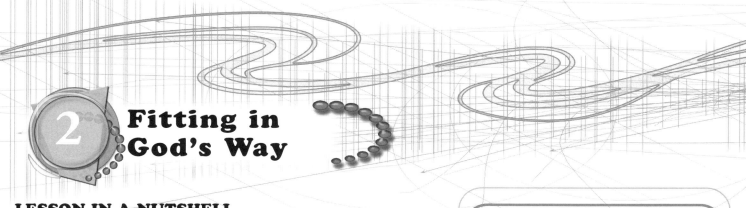

2 Fitting in God's Way

LESSON IN A NUTSHELL

Tweens are seeking acceptance from peers, adults, and their family. They desire to "fit in" and will seek to make that happen. They need to find ways to fit in that do not compromise who they are as children of God.

A PUZZLING PROBLEM (5–8 minutes)

As tweens arrive, have them work with one another to put together simple puzzles. They must stay at the first table they choose. They may not talk to those who are not at their table. They will be unable to complete the puzzles, because you have removed three or four of the central pieces (the ones that don't have a straight side) and switched them between puzzles. After all have arrived, invite the tweens to search among the other tables for the pieces that fit in their puzzle. Allow them to complete their puzzles—still without talking.

Say: **Sometimes choosing a group to belong to is not as simple as it seems.** Ask:

- How did you recognize that some of the pieces did not fit in with your puzzle? (*wrong color on back, different shape, wrong picture segment on front, would not fit anywhere*)
- What was your first response? (*throw it away; push it aside; become angry, frustrated, resentful*)
- What options did you have? (*make it fit, trade with another group, try to change the shape or color*)

Say: **We are like these puzzle pieces. Sometimes we find ourselves in places where we don't fit. These puzzle pieces did not have the choice of where they belong, but we do. Let's see what you might do in a similar situation.**

HOW FAR WOULD YOU GO? (10–20 minutes)

Invite the tweens to divide into groups of three or four. Provide the groups with the scenarios. Encourage the tweens to discuss how far they would go in each situation in order to fit in. Allow about half your allotted time for this portion of the discussion. Call time.

Ask for volunteers to talk about their small group's answers. Then have everyone back in their groups to discuss the possible

Before They Arrive

- ❑ Place different jigsaw puzzles on several tables, being sure to remove three or four pieces from each puzzle and placing them in other puzzle boxes.
- ❑ Make copies of the scenarios from page 13,
- ❑ Read the Scripture in advance; be sure you have a clear and comfortable way to answer questions tweens may have about the meaning of some of the words.

Supplies

- ❑ Bibles
- ❑ Several small tables or puzzle mats
- ❑ Simple jigsaw puzzles (one for every three to four tweens)
- ❑ Copies of scenarios from page 14
- ❑ Pencils and paper
- ❑ Cross that can be passed around a circle

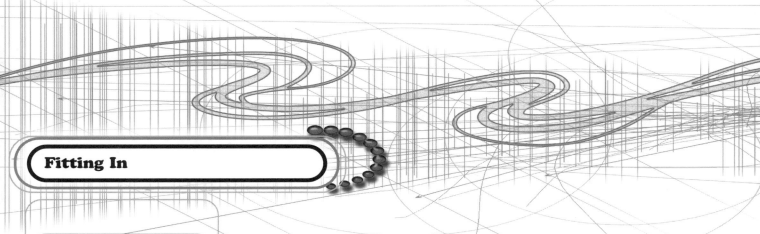

Fitting In

When Time Matters

If you have more time, for the activity **"It's Not Easy to Follow God's Word,** invite each group to choose a scenario to act out, showing their God's way responses and the possible consequences.

consequences of the actions they were willing to take. Allow about half your allotted time for this portion of the discussion. Call time and talk together about some of the consequences they identified.

WHAT DOES GOD SAY? (10 minutes)

Say: **Every situation presents us with options, but we don't always know what to do. One tool we have in knowing how to act in any situation is our relationship with God. God speaks to us through the Bible. Let's see what God has to say about fitting in.**

Have the tweens read **Colossians 3:1-17** (New life in Christ) and **Psalm 119:1-16** (Delight in God's ways) and make a list of the guidance given.

IT'S NOT EASY TO FOLLOW GOD'S WORD (5–20 minutes)

Invite the tweens to return to their small groups. Encourage them to discuss the scenarios again. This time they will discuss what they think God would want them to do in each situation. Encourage them to list the consequences of taking God's way. Encourage them to list people in their lives who would support their decision to take God's way.

SENDING FORTH (3–6 minutes)

Invite the tweens to participate in a prayer circle. Have them sit in a circle in chairs or on the floor. Provide a medium-size cross that the tweens can pass around the circle. Begin by saying: **We will close our time today with a prayer circle. As the cross is passed from person to person, the person holding the cross may pray out loud or silently. Please do not speak until you are holding the cross. I will begin and end the prayer circle. We will pass the cross around the circle two times. The first time around, pray for situations keeping people from fitting in. The second time around, pray for strength to respond to situations in God's way.**

You may wish to begin the prayer by honestly stating a situation in your own life in which you are feeling left out. The second time around, pray for strength to respond to the situation you presented. Finish with a prayer that God will give strength to each person sitting around that circle.

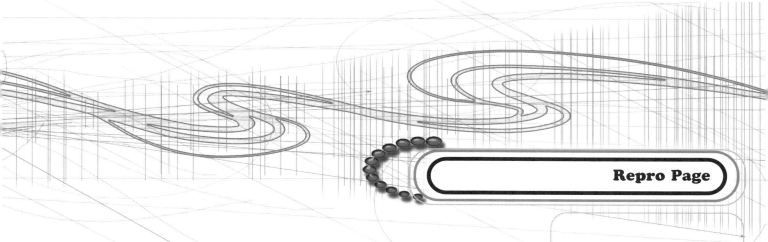

Scenarios

Directions

You will discuss these scenarios three different times with different questions, which your leader will give you.

1. Several students from your school are starting a club. All of your friends are talking about it. In order to be a member, you have to steal an article of clothing from an expensive store at the mall. Your friends ask you to join them for a "day at the mall." They want you to be a witness for their initiation into the new club.

2. Every day after school, a group of students walks home. Along the way, they always pass by the home of an older couple. This couple has a flower garden in their front yard. Several students decide to pick the flowers. They encourage you to come with them, calling you names for not wanting to participate.

3. Christmas is two weeks away, and you need money for presents for your friends. A local resale shop is offering to buy used Christmas decorations. Several of your friends are getting together tonight to walk the neighborhood in search of outdoor decorations that would be easy to steal. The plan is to take the decorations to the resale shop and split the money among those who participate.

4. School elections are scheduled for next week. Your best friend is running for Student Council and is afraid that he is going to lose. This election is very important to him. A group of students gathers at your house for a strategy session. As you discuss ways to campaign for your friend, someone suggests that the group begin telling lies about the other candidates. The conversation begins to get out of hand.

5. Your best friend's mother is a teacher at your school. One day you are at your friend's house and see the questions for the final exam lying on the kitchen counter. Everyone is expecting this test to be really hard. If you had the questions, you could pass them out at school. You would be the most popular person at school.

3 Fit for God

Before They Arrive

- ❑ Set the tables; make them festive as well as functional. Include nametags and markers, if needed, "favorite meal menus," food, disposable cameras to document the events of the day, place settings, pencils.
- ❑ Create a larger version of the Food Pyramid (page 18) on a large sheet of paper or posterboard.
- ❑ Write on sticky notes the names of the favorite foods or ingredients listed on the menus that the adults made.
- ❑ Write out on index cards or slips of paper the scrambled spelling for numerous healthful foods, especially fresh fruits and vegetables.
- ❑ Make copies for the group of the reproducible pages (pages 18–19).

LESSON IN A NUTSHELL

God has given us bodies. Eating well is an act of stewardship, of taking care of what God has entrusted to us. Taking care of ourselves physically is a way of honoring God. Assuring that others have adequate nutrition is also a way of honoring God.

GET READY

- ❑ Poll the tweens to find out whether any of them have serious food allergies so that you can avoid recipes featuring those foods. Also, find out about their food preferences. This knowledge will help you in your search for recipes they are sure to love.
- ❑ Several weeks in advance, look for cookbooks featuring healthful, delicious, kid-friendly recipes (preferably using seasonal ingredients). Bring some to the Tween Time.
- ❑ Plan with your adult leadership team or persons who have volunteered specifically for this event to prepare some of the recipes for the opening activity.
- ❑ Have your adults also write up "favorite meal menus" showing healthful choices—including tween favorites. Encourage the adults to be creative in making their menu look interesting. They may want to give the food item a fun name and then write a brief description of it, including some of the ingredients. Have the adults look at some restaurant menus for some ideas.
- ❑ Reserve the church dining area and kitchen for your gathering. Make sure that all the supplies you need are there. Review the church kitchen policies and safety procedures.
- ❑ Arrange transportation to take the tweens and the food they prepare to a local feed-the-hungry program.
- ❑ A week before the gathering or with a mid-week phone call or e-mail, tell tweens to wear clothing they do not mind getting dirty as they will be cooking during the gathering. Remind the tweens to bring their permission forms.
- ❑ Get fresh, locally grown or produced ingredients for the recipes and any supplies that you will need a few days before the gathering.

YOUR FAVORITE MEAL (15–20 minutes)

As the tweens arrive, direct them to the dining area, which should be festive and welcoming. Have them fill out nametags if they are

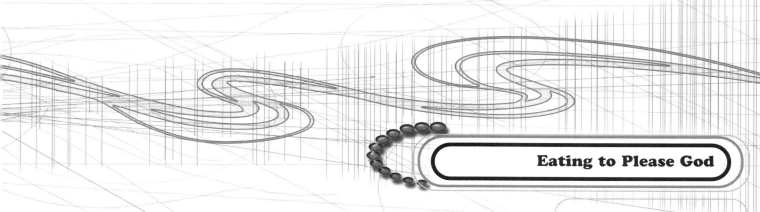

new to one another. On the tables will be your adult leaders' menus, napkins, place settings, various foods, paper, pencils, and disposable cameras for documenting the event.

Have one of the tweens offer or lead a blessing for the food; or sing together the Johnny Appleseed blessing, the Doxology, or another favorite. Invite the tweens to eat and to enjoy themselves at the table gathering. Encourage them to look at the menus. Tell them they may take pictures, but not to take all of them at this time; they need to save some for the rest of the event.

After the members of the group have a chance to eat, read the menus, socialize, and introduce the tweens to the New Food Pyramid. The New Food Pyramid outlines what people should eat to stay healthy. As part of the presentation, have the adults place their sticky notes of ingredients/recipes in the appropriate food category on the large food pyramid chart.

Then give the tweens their own copy of the New Food Pyramid (pages 18–19). Have them write several of their favorite foods, at least one in each category. For example, if cheese is a favorite, it would go in the Dairy section.

In small groups, each with an adult leader (or all together if the group is already small), find out what the tweens have written and ask questions such as these:

- Why do you like these foods?
- How do you feel after you eat them?
- Describe how one of your favorite foods is prepared.

Adult leaders may also talk about their favorite healthful foods, noting that these foods give them energy and make them more productive at work. They may also tell stories of persons who who have suffered from diseases as a result of poor nutrition, poor eating habits, and non-healthful food preparation methods (for example, diabetes, cancer, heart disease, and of course, obesity, which contributes to all kinds of health and mobility problems). Group leaders will stress the need for caring for their bodies for the sake of good health by eating a balanced diet, three meals (not skipping breakfast), and moderate portions.

NAME THAT FOOD GROUP (5–7 minutes)

Use masking tape to reproduce a very large, empty food pyramid shape on the floor (see margin and pages 18–19). Give each tween an index card on which you have written the scrambled spelling for the name of various healthful foods. Each tween will need to unscramble his or her word, tape it to himself or herself, and then stand on the correct spot on the large floor food pyramid.

Supplies

- [ ] Bibles
- [ ] Paper. pens, pencils
- [ ] Sticky notes
- [ ] Markers
- [ ] Large sheets of paper

- [ ] Favorite Meal Menus (see page 14)
- [ ] Food from Group Leader's Favorite Meal
- [ ] The New Food Pyramid
- [ ] Blank New Food Pyramid

- [ ] Disposable cameras for the tweens to use throughout the fellowship experience
- [ ] Packaging for food to take to the feeding program.

Food Pyramid Example

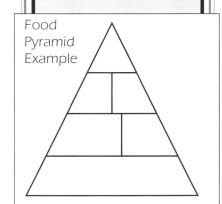

Make the floor pyramid large enough for the number of participants. If you
have a large numbers of kids, you may need to have more than one food in
one or more categories of the food pyramid.

Then, each tween group will be assigned to learn about one food group.
Each group will peruse kid-friendly, healthful cookbooks in search of dishes
they'd like to prepare and eat. (The cookbooks can be obtained from your
local library or from your local bookstore.) In addition, each group will review
recipes selected by the group leaders to be prepared during today's fellowship
gathering.

Don't forget to take photographs.

GET MOVING! (10–15 minutes)

After all of the emphasis on eating, it is important to incorporate some
physical exercise as part of your program, helping tweens understand that
exercise can be fun.

Have available the equipment needed for some locally popular active game,
such as Four-Square, Frisbee®, an active relay race, or an obstacle course you
have set up ahead of time. If you are limited to inside space, you can play a
game such as Upset the Fruit Basket or let tweens dance to some lively music.

LOOK A LITTLE DEEPER (10–20 minutes)

Gather the tweens again. Ask:

- What do you think eating good food and getting exercise has to do with
  God?

Accept and affirm their responses without moving them to a "right" answer.
The purpose of the question is to get the tweens thinking.

Invite the tweens to hear the story of Daniel and his three friends. As an
introduction to the story, say: **Daniel and his friends were among the
people of Jerusalem who had been conquered by the Babylonians.
They were taken away from their homeland to live in Babylonia. This
time was called the Exile; the people were under the strict rule of
their conquerors and were not allowed to go home. Daniel and his
three friends were among several of the Jewish captives who were
chosen for special favor. They were to be fed lavishly and prepared for
service in the king's palace. That doesn't sound like such a bad thing!**

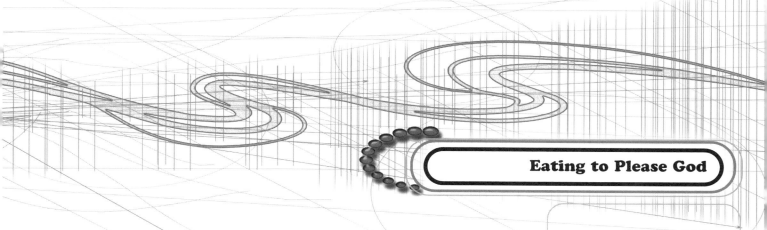

However, Daniel and his friends wanted to remain faithful to God even in a new land. As Jews, they observed health and dietary practices, which they understood to be what God desired for them. To accept the wine and rich foods from the king was to go against their loyalty to God and to "defile" themselves, making them unfit to serve God. But they were captives and the king was in charge.

Tell them to read **Daniel 1:8-20** to find out the rest of the story.

Ask:

- How hard do you think it would be to be faithful to God in a situation in which someone else had power over you? in which you had to go against what seemed like a really good deal? Have you ever experienced such a situation?
- Why would God care about what people eat today? (*God made us; God loves us; God desires that we are healthy*.)
- How do you feel about eating differently from those around you?
- How do you think Daniel felt?
- What helped Daniel to stand up for doing what he thought was right? (*his faith in God; his having friends who also believed and were with him*)

You may also note during the discussion that Daniel made a choice to follow God's way and to live a healthful life. God extends that choice to each of us, as well.

MAKE A FEAST (30–45 minutes)

Invite the tweens to prepare healthful dishes. Make sure that the tweens know kitchen safety procedures; and supervise their use of the equipment, especially knives. Have the group make enough for a taste for themselves and package most of the food to take to a local feed-the-hungry program. Remind the tweens to take photographs. Engage everyone in clean up.

SENDING FORTH (5–30 minutes)

Gather the tweens; Ask them to each tell something they learned about eating to please God or something else they learned from the Bible story. Then have the group bless the food and the people who will receive it, including themselves.

Eat together, do a final clean up, and then deliver the food to a nearby feed-the-hungry program.

Special Tips

The tweens and their adult leaders can create a photo diary of their healthy eating experiences and post them on the church's website or on a bulletin board. They may also want to post the menus and recipes so that other tween or youth groups may do what they have done.

When Time Matters

If time is short, have one of the adults deliver the food instead of taking the whole group.

The Food Guide Pyramid
(Developed by the USDA)

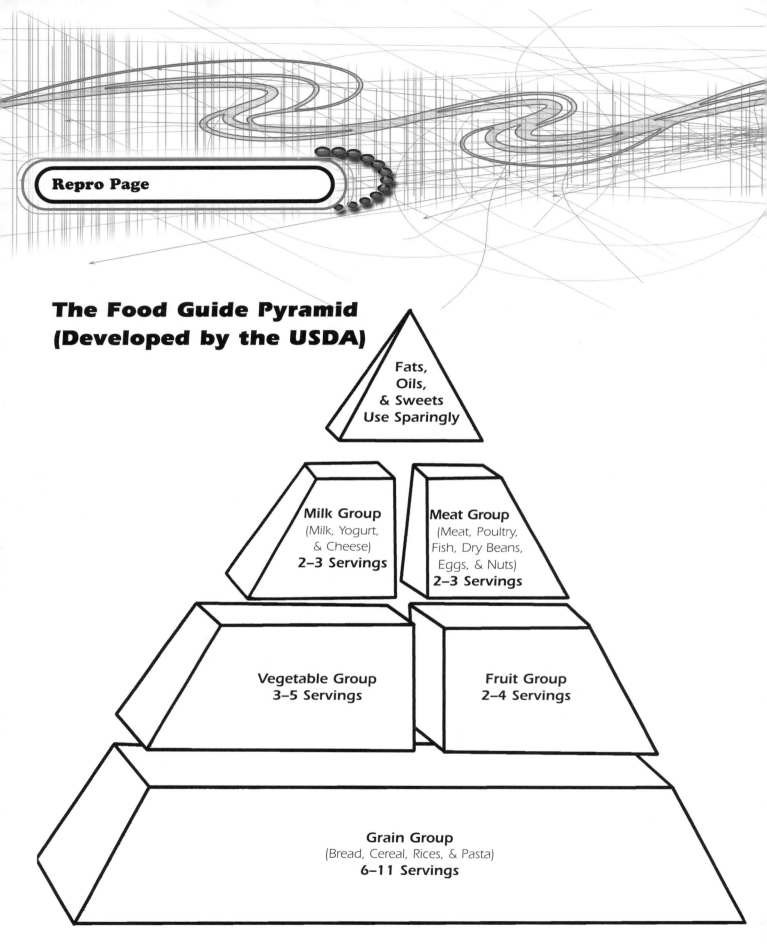

Fats,
Oils,
& Sweets
Use Sparingly

Milk Group
(Milk, Yogurt,
& Cheese)
2–3 Servings

Meat Group
(Meat, Poultry,
Fish, Dry Beans,
Eggs, & Nuts)
2–3 Servings

Vegetable Group
3–5 Servings

Fruit Group
2–4 Servings

Grain Group
(Bread, Cereal, Rices, & Pasta)
6–11 Servings

The Food Guide Pyramid (Developed by the USDA)

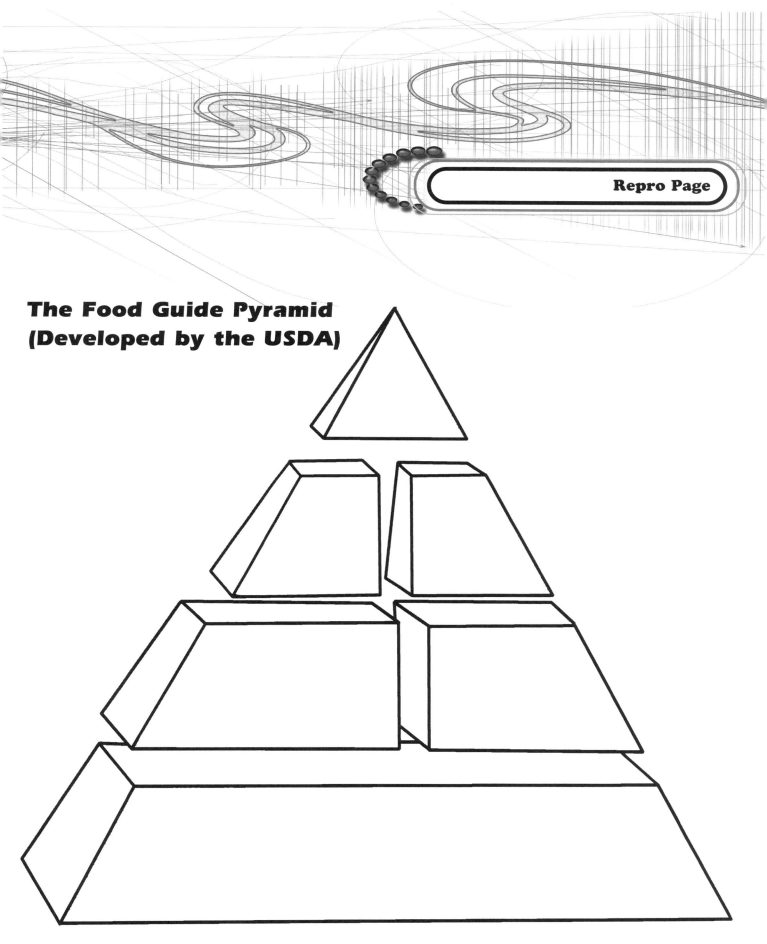

4 Stand Up for Right

LESSON IN A NUTSHELL

This lesson examines the pressure tweens face when their friends get caught up in questionable activities and helps tweens find the courage to stand apart.

LEGAL OR ILLEGAL? (10–15 minutes)

As tweens arrive, give them a sheet of paper and a copy of repro page 23 to respond to. When individuals have finished writing their answers, put them into groups of three or four to talk about what they wrote. Encourage them to talk through any answers about which they disagree.

Then go over the scenarios with the group. Engage them in brief conversation about why each scenario is legal or illegal (see the margin on page 21). Also, stress the importance of thinking before acting because activity without thinking can lead to more trouble than they could imagine.

TUG-O-WAR (5–10 minutes)

Get the rope and put half the tweens on one side and half on the other. Ask for a volunteer to stand in between the groups.

Tell each group that they are fighting for a part of a neighborhood to be their turf. Tell your volunteer that they are friends with people in each group or gang and it is their job to convince the groups not to fight. Instruct them that they are only to tug on the rope when they give their reason why they must get the turf. And, your volunteer in the middle can tug on the rope when he or she has something to say to convince the groups differently.

First allow the groups to practice tugging on the rope safely and then tell them to start their bickering.(If it appears that your volunteer is waning, jump in to help; or jump in to help anyway.) Allow the tug-o-war to go on for a few minutes and then have everyone sit where they are, still holding the rope.

Supplies

- ❏ Bibles
- ❏ Rope long enough to accommodate your whole group holding on (approximately 2 feet per participant); or do the activity more than once if your group is larger than your available rope
- ❏ Photocopies of Legal or Illegal? (page 23)
- ❏ Pencils or pens
- ❏ Plain paper
- ❏ Large white candle
- ❏ Small votive or tea light individual candles (as many as there are tweens and adults).
- ❏ Matches or a lighter; a candle lighter such as used by acolytes

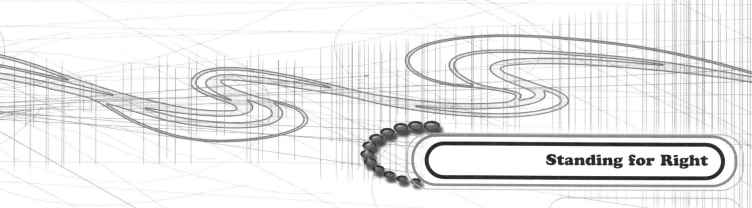

Ask the volunteer:

- Was it easier or harder to try to resolve this conflict and hold on with or without help?

Ask your groups:

- What was it like to have someone in the middle tugging and trying to resolve this battle?
- Did having a middle person make it harder to fight?
- Did anyone try to ignore the middle person?
- Did what the middle person gave as reasons not to fight make sense?
- Ask each group how they felt when the middle person got help?

Say: **Having friends or being part of a gang can be great, but sometimes our friends or gang pull us into activities that are not right in God's sight or in the eyes of the law. It's tough to stand up against things that are wrong when our friends are involved. Sometimes we're afraid to say anything or to walk away because they are our friends and we might lose them. But we have another Friend to help us in difficult situations.**

LOOK A LITTLE DEEPER (5–7 minutes)
Have a tween read aloud **Ephesians 6:10-11.** Ask:

- What do you think the "wiles of the devil" means? (*things that have some positive characteristics—such as keeping one's friends—but that will ultimately entrap persons in something very negative*)

Talk about the fact that when we are in a situation such as the ones on the reproducible page, we are likely to have a sense of those things being wrong, but we want to keep our friends; and so it is easy to give in to the pressure. Like the person in the tug-o-war, we need help—and we have help from God.

Read aloud **Ephesians 6:14-15**. Ask:

- In the situations from the repro page, how would "truth" and "righteousness" help a person stand up for what is right? (*Naming an action truthfully as harmful and wrong is a first step toward refusing to participate in it.*)

Say: **As followers of Christ, we are to "proclaim the gospel of peace." That means we are to help people know a way of being with one another that is good and right.**

Answers to Page 23

1. Legal—but not nice
2. Illegal—Spreading untruths about anyone that can be perceived by others as the truth is called "defamation of character," which can put you and your parents in the position to be sued. Most schools do not tolerate it either; you could be suspended or expelled.
3. Illegal—Vandalism of private or public property is against the law in any state.
4. Legal—However, if the "smaller kid" were to be physically harmed, this is called "assault"; and you could be charged as an accessory.
5. Illegal in most areas
6. Illegal—If you witness a crime being committed by someone you are "hanging out" with and he or she is caught, you could be charged as an accessory. In this case, you would be an accessory to petty theft.

21

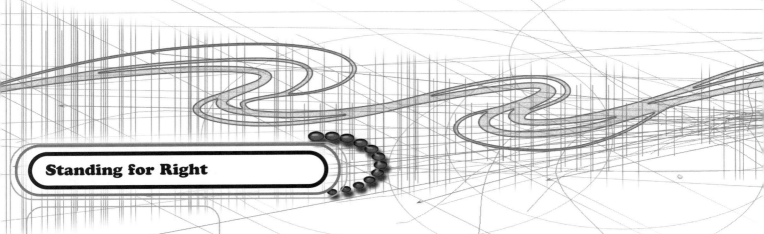

Refusal Skills

- Name the act as harmful and wrong. (That's shoplifting; it's wrong.)

- Offer a positive alternative. (I'd rather go get something to eat.)

- If not accepted, walk away. (I'm not doing that. See you later.)

PRACTICE WEARING THE ARMOR (10–20 minutes)

The armor of God includes truth and righteousness. Basic refusal skills start with naming something as wrong. Then the person can offer an alternative. If that is not accepted, he or she needs to walk away. To do these things is not easy, but practice and encouragement from a community of Christians help.

Have the tweens divide into small groups of four or five and choose one of the scenarios from "Legal or Illegal?" sheet to roleplay. Or you may assign a specific one to each group. Or choose one to work through together.

Start the roleplay with reading the scenario. Then focus the dialogue on the refusal skills.

Together, talk about how having other Christians as friends can help us stand up against pressures and temptations to do wrong.

SENDING FORTH (2–5 minutes)

Gather before an altar, which has on it one large white candle and as many small votive or tea light candles as there are tweens. Dim the lights if possible. Ask your tweens to think of a situation or something that happened recently that they knew was wrong and either participated in or just did nothing.

Light the large candle.

Say: **When we think of standing up for what is right, it's easy to feel like we are the only light in a dark room. What difference do we make? But let's see what happens when each person makes a commitment to stand for right.**

Invite each tween to come forward, draw a flame from the large candle, light one individual candle, and return to his or her place. Be sure to monitor the lighting for safety.

Say: **When we draw our courage from God and we stand together, supporting one another in doing what is right and good, we do indeed make a difference!**

Lead your tweens in a prayer asking God to give us all courage when we feel pressure to do things that are not right.

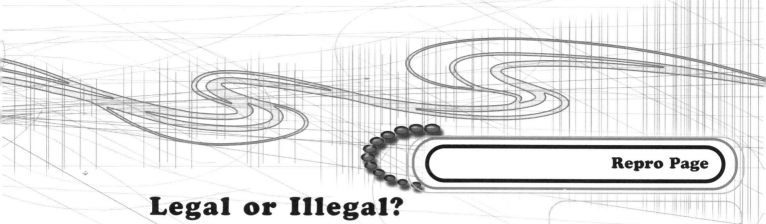

Legal or Illegal?

Directions

Circle whether the action is legal or illegal.

When you finish, find another person or two to talk about your answers. Tell why you chose the answer you did. Are there any answers you disagree with?

1. You and your friends tease an acquaintance about how his or her clothes look until you succeed in upsetting him or her.

   Legal   Illegal

2. You and your friends, for "fun," start spreading untrue rumors about someone at school.

   Legal   Illegal

3. You and your friends are a clique or gang and have decided to call yourselves the Rude Dawgs, so you spray paint this name on your lockers at school.

   Legal   Illegal

4. You watch your friends teasing and physically picking on a kid smaller than they are. You do not stop them, nor do you go and tell an adult.

   Legal   Illegal

5. You and your friends decide to buy pocketknives and carry them at school and in your neighborhood.

   Legal   Illegal

6. You and your friends go to a convenience store. You buy some candy, but you witness one of your friends stealing a bag of potato chips. However, you do not tell the store clerk.

   Legal   Illegal

Special Place Prayer Time
5

Before They Arrive

❑ Assemble indoor picnic items and create a picnic atmosphere in the social hall.
❑ Have sheets of white or construction paper for sketching and drawing.
❑ Have an assortment of colored pencils, crayons, magic markers, or paints and brushes available for drawing and sketching.

Supplies

❑ Bibles
❑ "Picnic blankets," large pillows, paper plates, napkins, and so on
❑ Foods can vary from light, healthful finger foods to traditional picnic fare. Whatever fits your time, energy, and budget will be fine.
❑ Music for stretching exercises (optional)
❑ Nature sounds CD or audiocassette (optional)
❑ CD player or cassette player (optional)
❑ Large sheets of paper or construction paper
❑ Markers, colored pencils, crayons, paints, and paint supplies

LESSON IN A NUTSHELL

The tweens will learn about Jesus' need to retreat to a place where he could be alone with God to pray. They will experience a prayerful retreat of their own.

INDOOR PICNIC (15–20 minutes)

As the tweens arrive, direct them to your "picnic" area. Invite them to sit and enjoy the food and fellowship. Welcome them to the gathering. After a time of socializing and munching (and clean up), have an adult leader guide the tweens in some stretching exercises. Start with some more high energy and fun stretches and then move to ones that begin to quiet the group and prepare them for the imagination exercise. You may want to use music as part of the stretching time.

Or have the group pretend to be trees in the picnic area that are blown by the wind. Continue with that idea and have the tweens create a "rainstorm." They can snap their fingers in intervals to simulate light sprinkles, then faster for more "rain drops." They can create "thunder" and a hard "storm" (stomping as well as snapping) and then have the "rain" ease up (back to snapping fingers only).

JUST IMAGINE (4–6 minutes)

Invite the tweens to sit, relax, and close their eyes. They are to imagine the perfect outdoor picnic spot or a place in the natural world they would find special.

You may want to do a guided visualization, asking them (with pauses between) what they see in their perfect spot, what they hear as they listen, and what smells are there. Use music on CD or audiocassette with sounds from nature, if desired. Encourage the tweens to imagine every detail.

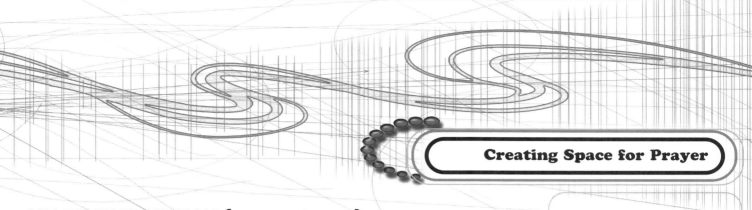

SHARE YOUR VISION (15–25 minutes)

Once the tweens have imagined this perfect place, invite them to draw or paint what they saw in their mind's eye; continue playing music if you have it.

Gather the tweens; invite volunteers to tell about their drawings, their special place.

JESUS NEEDED A RETREAT TOO (10–20 minutes)

Say: **Picnics and other escapes to nature offer people a chance to rest, dream, pray, socialize, laugh, and have fun. Finding a special place in the outdoors feeds people's souls. Jesus, also, went to nature to be renewed. There he could rest, problem-solve, pray, and give thanks to God so that he could keep doing God's work.**

Together examine the Scriptures that describe Jesus' retreating to the natural world. Read aloud **Matthew 14:13** (Jesus withdrew after hearing of the death of John the Baptist). Ask:

- Why do you think Jesus wanted to be alone with God after he heard about the death of John the Baptist?
- When you experience something sad, how do you react? What helps you?

Read aloud **Mark 1:35** (Jesus prayed in the early morning). Have the tweens look also at verses 32-34 and then verses 36-39. Ask:

- Why do you think Jesus took time to go pray? He could have just slept in.
- How do you set aside time for prayer? Do you have a special place or time?

Read aloud **Matthew 26:36** (Jesus prayed in the garden of Gethsemane). Invite the tweens to fill in the context of this passage. (After the Lord's Supper, Jesus prayed in the garden, knowing that he would be betrayed, suffer, and die.) Ask:

- When you are facing something very difficult, how do you handle your fears or hurt?
- Has anyone ever asked you to pray for him or her? What do you do?

Notes

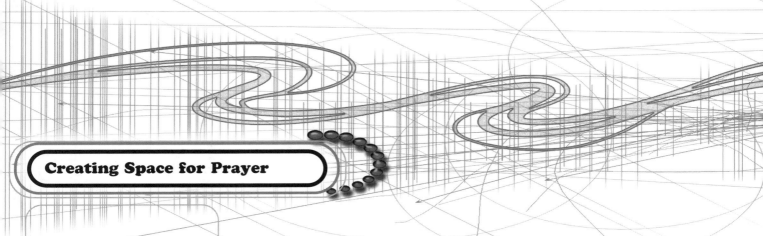

Creating Space for Prayer

Say: **Jesus found it important to find time to be alone with God. As Christians we follow Jesus' example as we make the practice of prayer important to us.**

PRAYER TIME (7–10 minutes)

Have the tweens take their drawing of their special spot to some place within the area where they can have individual space, not close to others. They may take a pillow or a "picnic blanket" as well. Invite them to use the silence with their drawing as a focal point, to create a special place for this prayer time. Tell them that they will have about five minutes of silence and that you will call them together when the time comes.

They may pray about whatever is on their mind or heart.

SENDING FORTH (3–5 minutes)

Call the group together; invite them to place their drawings in the center of their closing circle.

Say: **God has given us beautiful places, special places where we can feel renewed. God invites us to enter those special places and find God there. We can trust God to be with us and to hear our prayers. Go in peace.**

Special Tips

Encourage the tweens to take their drawings home. If there are any left, you may wish to post in the room.

26

6 Family Matters

LESSON IN A NUTSHELL

A divorce means a big change in the lives of tweens. This lesson will help them know that they are still a part of a family, that talking about how they feel is the best way to heal, and that God is a great listener who continues to work in their lives for good.

BUILDING AND REBUILDING (10–15 minutes)

Divide tweens into teams of three or four. Give each group at least 15 to 20 cards. Tell the tweens to build whatever they want with the cards.

Of course, it will be hard for their structures to stay built; so after they have struggled for a few minutes, offer glue sticks. Then allow a few more minutes for them to create their structure.

Briefly discuss how when it seems that nothing in life is going right. (*Give tween examples such as dislike a teacher at school, has a lot of homework, can't get along with siblings, can't hang out with an older sibling, parents not getting along.*) God is the glue that can hold everything together or put things back together.

CORRESPONDENCE (8–12 minutes)

Give the tweens a sheet of paper and a pen or pencil and tell them to write the date somewhere on the paper and that is all.

Then ask the tweens how their week was? Did they have many challenges? What went great? What went wrong? Inform them that they are to answer these questions as if writing a letter to a friend. Tell them they may write to a real friend or an imaginary one. Ask them how they identify their friends. Whom do they confide in or tell their secrets to? Have them all open their letters with "Dear Friend" or the actual name of their friend.

Instruct the tweens to write to their friend about whatever challenges they had and to ask their friend for help. Encourage the tweens to be as specific as possible when asking for help. Remind them that when they close their letters, they should thank their friend for supporting them. Put the letters aside for now.

BLENDING IN (10–15 minutes)

Ask the tweens how they would define the word *family.* Give volunteers a dictionary and have them read aloud the various definitions and compare them.

Divide the tweens into groups of no more than four or five persons; assign them one or more of the scenarios from page 30. Instruct the tweens that each group is to discuss the components of the family in their assigned scenario. Refer the groups to the directions and discussion questions on the repro page handout.

Have each group come up with at least two reasons why their scenario is a family. Encourage them to come up with more reasons if they can. Invite each group to read their scenario and explain why it describes a family.

Affirm families, related or created, in whatever form they take.

DIVORCE—WHO CARES? (5–15 minutes)

Here is a suggestion for tackling the subject of divorce. However, the make-up of your group should be your guide. Keep in mind that statistically, about half of all marriages end in divorce. Some of your tweens may have experienced it; others may be in the middle of a divorce; still others may experience it in the future. (See Special Tips also.)

You may wish to introduce the topic of divorce by talking about change and the fact that life is full of changes. Ask your tweens how they feel about changes that happen in their lives? Are some changes good? Have they experienced changes that are bad but that also have some good?

Mention that sometimes marriages change. Once divorce is brought up, then talk about how a family can change if there is a divorce. Some persons may feel that the family unit has been destroyed. Focus the discussion on the fact that the family is not ruined, but it is being restructured. Divorce will require change; change is hard, but it can also have some good as a part of it.

Remind the tweens that a divorce is not their fault and that, in the strain of a troubled marriage or a divorce, parents are not intentionally ignoring the children. Parents have a lot on their mind. Bring in the idea that in such situations, the young persons may need to start conversation with Mom and/or Dad. They may also write to Mom or Dad to express their needs and fears. Or they may need to find another trusted adult to talk with about the confusion, hurt, and anger they have about the divorce. Encourage the tweens to seek help and to talk about their feelings and concerns.

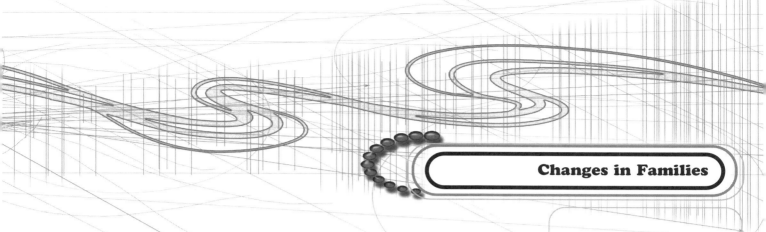

Remind the tweens that, although life changes, God is unchanging, God's love is steadfast, and God is present to them always. Refer the tweens to the letter they wrote to a friend earlier. Ask the tweens to consider "What if the friend in your letter were God?" Point out that they can talk to God whenever they need to. One way is to write God a letter just as they did earlier to a friend.

Briefly discuss with the tweens the similarities between their letter to God and a prayer to God. Are there any differences?

LOOK A LITTLE DEEPER (10–15 minutes)

Ask a volunteer to read aloud **Romans 8:28.** Encourage the tweens to say what they think the Scripture passage means. (*It does not mean that God makes all things happen; it does mean that God continues to work in all things toward good. Those who love God, who respond to God by working toward God's purposes of love and justice will see God at work in their lives in the midst of "all things," including suffering.*)

Ask the tweens to think of situations where God has made things "work together" because God loves us. How do we feel supported? How does God support us?

Encourage the tweens to memorize this verse. Remind them that our role as "those who love God" is to look for and to trust that God is at work in "all things," good or bad.

SENDING FORTH (2–5 minutes)

Have the tweens get their letters and tell them to quickly change the friend's name to God. Then encourage them to find their own personal space in the room where they can sit quietly and comfortably alone.

If you desire, play some inspirational music softly in the background. Instruct the tweens to read their letters to God to themselves and have a time of personal prayer.

Once it appears that everyone has read his or her letter to God and has been in prayer, have the tweens stay where they are and close with this or a similar prayer:

God, we thank you for our families, in whatever form they take. Thank you also for being with us when all else is changing. Help us see you at work for good in the midst of our tough times. Amen.

When Time Matters

If you have more time, give the tweens the following psalms to look up, pick their favorite or the one that best speaks to them, and make themselves a book mark with the construction paper provided.

Psalm 36:7
Psalm 46:1-2a
Psalm 121:1-2

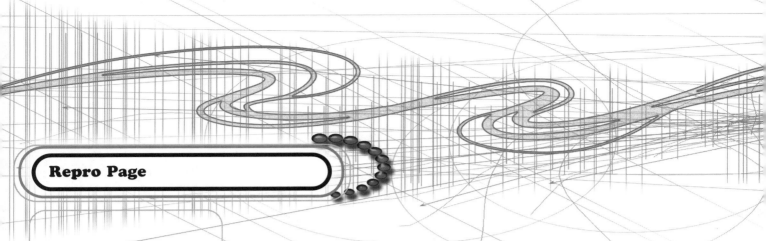

Family Scenarios

Directions

Discuss your particular scenario(s):

- How is this family different from the traditional family?

- How is it similar?

- What makes this scenario a family?

Come up with *at least* two reasons why the people in this scenario are a family.

Be ready to read your assigned scenario and explain why it is a family.

1. I have never met my father. I live with my mom. After school everyday, I walk to my grandma's and I stay there until my mom picks me up after she gets off work. But I don't have much of a family.

2. I live with my parents.

3. During the week I'm either at my mom's or my dad's. I spend alternate weekends with each of them. When I'm at my mom's, we go to Shine Your Light Church. I have lots of friends there. My mom and Miss Priscilla have been friends for four years. They kind of look a like. They tell everybody that they are sisters. I am good friends with her kids, Jasmine and Jonathan. But I don't have much of a family.

4. I live with my aunt and uncle and three cousins. I share a room with my cousin, Bernie. People think we are brothers, but I tell them we are not. Every Sunday after church we go the Simpsons' house and eat Sunday dinner. My aunt usually brings something she cooked, too. The Simpsons are good friends of my aunt and uncle. Anyway, I don't have much of a family.

5. I live with my grandmother. It's just me and Granny. The rest of our family live in Chicago and Iowa. We don't get to see them much. I like spending time with my granny. We go to the movies, do chores together, play cards, and just sit and talk. It's just me and Granny; we're not much of a family.

6. I live with my dad. I visit my mom every weekend. My dad is married again, so I have a step-mom and two step-siblings, Tre' and Porscha. My mom is married again too. I have a step-dad and a step-brother who is older than me. I love being at either house even though I don't have much of a family.

7. It's just me, my mom, and my two younger sisters. My sisters and I have different fathers. Every summer we separate to go visit our fathers' mothers (our grandmothers). Because we all three have different fathers and grannies, we are not much of a family.

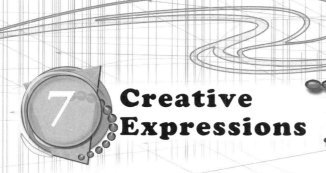

Creative Expressions

LESSON IN A NUTSHELL

Tweens learn in different ways, and tweens have the gift of creativity. This experience offers tweens the opportunity to understand and enjoy Scripture in creative ways.

SCRIPTURE HUNT (5–8 minutes)

As tweens arrive, invite them to participate in a search for their Scripture. Prior to your meeting, copy the Scripture search cards, cut them apart, and hide them around the room. Instruct the tweens to search the room for a Scripture card. When they find one, they are to go to the Bible and find that Scripture. They are then to read the passage and write on the card short phrases about the meaning of that Scripture for their lives.

CREATIVE SCRIPTURES (15–25 minutes)

Divide the tweens into groups based upon the Scripture they found in the hunt. Have them tell one another their words or phrases about that Scripture. After all have spoken, have them work together in pairs, small groups (three to five), or individually to create their own expression of that Scripture and its meaning. They will later present it to the entire group.

Point out the stations and supplies you have set up for them:

- **Movement:** Provide tweens with a variety of scarves, rhythm instruments, and other similar items.

- **Music:** Provide tweens with a variety of musical instruments.

- **Drama:** Provide tweens with costumes and props.

- **3-D Collage or Sculpture:** Provide tweens with a box of mismatched items such as those found in that catch-all kitchen drawer (old keys, pieces of wood, cast off plastic items, buttons, lace trims, plus glue or wire, and so forth).

- **Art:** Provide tweens with large sheets of paper and a variety of artistic media (paper, crayons, markers, paints and brushes, clay)

Before They Arrive

- ❏ Gather supplies needed for the creative stations.
- ❏ Set up stations throughout the room.
- ❏ Copy on index cards or slips of paper the Scripture Search References at the bottom of page 32; hide them around the room.
- ❏ Make copies of the closing litany "Thanks, God!" (page 33) for each tween or post it on a large sheet of paper or posterboard.

Supplies

- ❏ Bibles
- ❏ Scripture search cards
- ❏ Pencils
- ❏ Scarves, rhythm instruments
- ❏ Musical instruments
- ❏ Costumes
- ❏ Junk items for sculpture, glue, wire
- ❏ Large sheet of paper or posterboard
- ❏ Large sheets of paper, poster or fingerpaints, brushes, watercolors, crayons, markers, clay, water cups for paints, old shirts to protect clothing

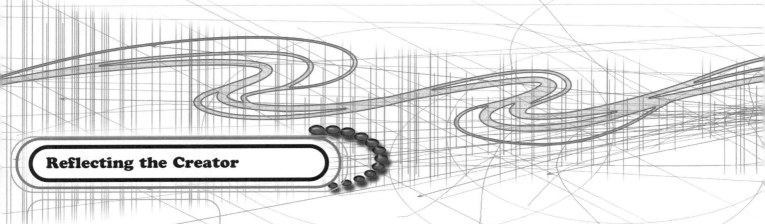

Special Tips

Look for ways to present the tweens' creative expressions of Scripture to a larger audience, such as creating a church hallway art exhibition or presenting them to a group of younger children or at a larger church event.

The expressions may also be appropriate for worship. Check with the pastor or worship coordinator about presenting them as part of congregational worship.

WHAT DOES GOD SAY? (3–5 minutes)

Have one of the tweens read aloud **Genesis 1:1-2.** Have other tweens read aloud **Psalm 24:1-2** and **Psalm 33:6-9.**

Say: **God is the creator of the universe and all that is in it. God gives each of us the gift of creativity, which shows in different ways. We are privileged to use our creativity to share God's word with others.**

SHARING OUR CREATIVE SCRIPTURES (8–20 minutes)

Invite each small group to present their creative expressions of Scripture to the larger group. Be sure to affirm each effort.

SENDING FORTH (3–6 MINUTES)

Say: **Today we experienced the joy of creation. God gives each one of us the ability to express our ideas in a variety of ways. By creatively expressing our understanding of Scripture we come to a better understanding of God's Word for ourselves and for others. Let's thank God for creativity and the freedom of expression.**

Divide the group into two groups to say the litany on page 33.

Scripture Search References

Copy these references or other favorites onto slips of paper or index cards, and hide them in the room.

Genesis 7:1-5	The Charge to Noah
Matthew 2:13-18	Baby Jesus Escapes to Egypt
Mark 16:1-8	The Resurrection
Luke 9:10-17	Feeding of the Multitude
Luke 24:13-33	The Road to Emmaus
Acts 21:13-44	The Shipwreck of Paul

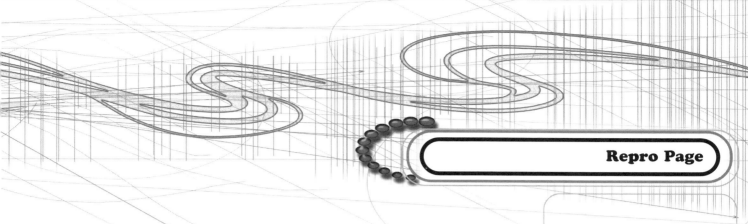

Thanks, God!

ALL: Thanks, God,

Group 1: for sharing your awesome Word with us.

ALL: Thanks, God,

Group 2: for giving us our own creativity.

ALL: Thanks, God,

Group 1: for letting us be free to express ourselves.

ALL: Thanks, God,

Group 2: for accepting what we create.

ALL: Thanks, God,

Group 1: for allowing us to share your Word through art, music, drama, and dance.

ALL: Thanks, God,

Group 2: for allowing us to share your Word through our words and actions.

ALL: Thanks, God,

Group 1: for allowing us to look at your Word in new ways and be willing to share it.

ALL: Thanks, God!

Group 2: Thanks for being with us.

ALL: Amen.

Directions

Are you truly thankful for the gifts God has given you?

Then shout it out!

Whenever ALL are to speak, join your voices with enthusiasm. Let everyone know!

8 Skunk or Turtle?

Before They Arrive

❏ Prior to today's session, gather pictures of situations around the world that elicit a response. Look in a variety of news magazines to find photos of world situations.

❏ Post each picture on a large sheet of paper. Provide pens or markers for tweens to write "graffiti" on the paper beside or below each picture.

Supplies

❏ Bibles,
❏ Large sheets of paper
❏ Photos of world events
❏ Markers
❏ Copies of "I'm Angry!" page 36

LESSON IN A NUTSHELL

Anger is not in and of itself a bad emotion, but some expressions of anger can have bad consequences. Tweens will learn positive ways to deal with anger.

WHAT AM I FEELING? (5–8 minutes)

As tweens arrive, invite them to look at the pictures posted around the room. What feelings do these pictures evoke in them? Encourage the tweens to write these feelings on the paper beside or below each picture—graffiti style.

Have the tweens quickly review all of the pictures and then gather. Say: **One of the feelings that situations like these often bring out is anger. Anger can be good if it helps us get things clear and moves us toward making things better. However, anger can also have some unwanted consequences.**

SKUNK OR TURTLE? (10–15 minutes)

Divide tweens into groups of three to five. The groups are to show how a skunk and a turtle are like people who are angry. They may do so with a quick skit or demonstration or by drawing an illustration. Those who choose to draw may also add words to their picture. To get them started, ask them to imagine themselves: When you get angry, are you more like a skunk or a turtle?

Have the groups present their analogies. Pick up on the tweens' comparisons; make these points if they do not bring them out:

A skunk's reaction to something is to spray and run away. The result is a mess that smells up everything for a long time. When people "blow up" out of anger, sometimes that makes working things out more difficult.

A turtle's reaction is to withdraw and wait until things settle down. Then the turtle moves on. If persons who are angry never deal appropriately with the problem, that's not good either. But being a "turtle" long enough to think before acting can make it easier to deal with things and move on.

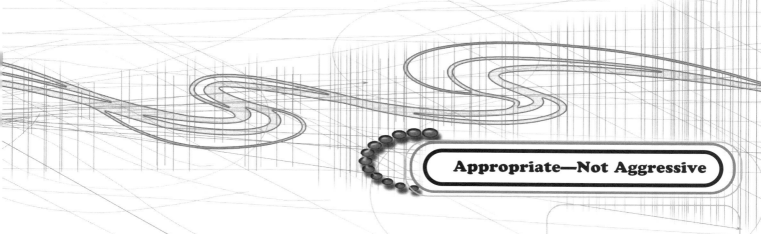

WHAT DOES GOD SAY? (5–15 minutes)

Have one of the tweens read aloud the Scripture lesson from **James 1:19-20.** Ask:

- What are some ways we can slow down our angry responses so that we are more like a turtle?
- Why do you think the Bible puts "be quick to listen" first? How does listening help situations that could be filled with anger?
- How can God help us be slow to anger?

DEALING WITH ANGER (10–25 minutes)

Send the tweens back into small groups. Provide everyone with a copy of "I'm Angry!" on page 36. Assign each group a different situation. (If necessary, assign multiple groups the same scenario.) Tell the groups to deal with the assigned scenario first; then they may tackle the next ones if they have time. Encourage them to think carefully about their assigned situation and explore it with some depth before reading another one. The questions are listed on the sheet.

SENDING FORTH (3–6 minutes)

Invite the tweens to name the things in their life they are angry about. Provide slips of paper and pencils on which the tweens may write the things or situations in their life they are angry about. Place these slips in a basket or bag. Gather the tweens around your worship area.

Say: **As I read the situations or things you are angry about, we will all say: "Help me to be quick to listen and slow to anger."**

As you remove a slip of paper, say: **Lord, I am angry about . . .** (read the paper). Say: **Help me to be quick to listen and slow to anger.**

When all of the slips have been read, have the group repeat these phrases after you:

Thanks, God, for hearing my prayer. (Repeat.)

Thanks, God, for helping me listen. (Repeat.)

Thanks, God, for all you do for me. (Repeat.)

Amen.

When Time Matters

If you have more time, have the small groups deal with all of the "I'm Angry!" scenarios.

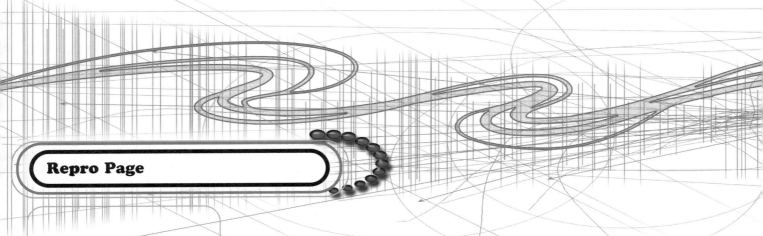

I'm Angry!

Directions

Read and deal with the scenarios first. If you finish, you may go on to another.

Here are some additional questions that may be helpful,

- Is your response more like a skunk or a turtle?

- What might be the consequences of your response?

- What did you want from this situation?

- Do you think that your response would accomplish your goal?

1. A group of students is standing outside the classroom. As you and your friend walk by, they call you insulting names. This has gone on every day for two weeks, and no one has stopped it. You have complained to the teacher and the principal. You are angry. How do you respond to the students? to the teacher and the principal?

2. One of your teachers has cancer. You and your classmates want to make a large get-well card to take to the hospital. The substitute teacher refuses to allow class time for this project. You will have to find some other way to get together. You are angry. How do you respond?

3. Your parents call a "family meeting." Your father has been offered a big promotion. However, it requires that your family move to a town more than 1,000 miles away. Your parents have made the decision to accept the promotion, and your family will be moving in four weeks. This is the first time you have heard about this. They did not ask your opinion. You are running for class president and have the lead in the school play, which takes place in six weeks. You are angry. How do you respond?

4. You have a specific table where you sit for lunch. Everyone knows that it is YOUR spot. You enter the lunchroom and find somebody else sitting at YOUR table. It's YOUR table! You are angry. How do you respond?

   Would you respond differently if the person were a new student? Why, or why not?

5. You studied hard for the first history test. Essay tests are difficult for you. When the test is returned, you find that the teacher has written several comments on your paper in letters big enough for nearby classmates to see. The comments are "This is not correct," "Improper use of information," and "Where did this come from?" You did the best you could. You are angry. How do you respond?

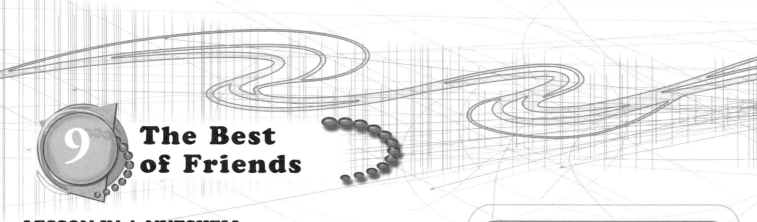

The Best of Friends

9

LESSON IN A NUTSHELL

This lesson helps tweens develop skills and attitudes that help them make and be good friends.

FUN FACTS (10–12 minutes)

As the tweens arrive, give them a copy of the Favorite Facts sheet (page 40). They are to find someone in the group to fill in a square and sign it. The only rule is that no one can sign a sheet twice unless it already includes the names of everyone else in the group.

Encourage the tweens to talk to each other as they gather the information. This activity is not a timed competition.

GETTING TO KNOW YOU (10 minutes)

At the end of your allotted time, assign each tween a partner. (If possible, connect pairs who do not know each other well.)

Have the partners find out from each other what from the sheet fits him or her (regardless of who signed the square). They are to use the information there as a starting point for getting to know each other better. They may expand their conversation in any direction as a follow up to what is on the sheet. The purpose is to find out more about the person, so additional questions are great. The tweens should also be looking for interests or experiences they have in common that they did not previously know that they did.

Tell the tweens that they will have about eight (or ten) minutes to find out as much as possible about each other. Let them know that you will tell them when they get to the half way mark, so they can be sure to give each partner time.

LET ME INTRODUCE YOU TO MY FRIEND (15–20 minutes)

Once time is up, convene the group as a whole, but have partners sit near each other. Ask volunteers to introduce their partner to the group, telling their partner's name and something they found out that they think is cool about that person.

Before They Arrive

- ❑ Make enough copies of the two repro pages for your tweens.
- ❑ Put the balls, pencils, cotton balls, and water bottles out of sight until you need them.

Supplies

- ❑ Bibles
- ❑ Unsharpened pencils
- ❑ Balls of any size
- ❑ Cotton balls
- ❑ Water bottles (either empty or full)
- ❑ Pens and pencils
- ❑ Copies of repro pages

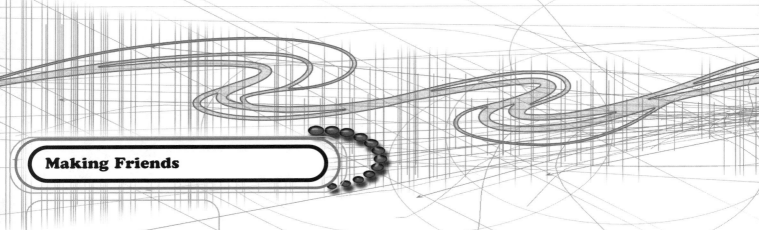

Making Friends

JUST DO IT! (10–15 minutes)

Have your partners from the previous activity be partners again. Tell them to sit on the floor, facing each other. Place a ball, pencil, cotton ball, and water bottle (either empty or full—but closed tight) in front of each pair.

Tell them that starting from their seated positions each set of partners must, without using their hands, stand up together while holding the item between them. Tell the tweens that they may hold the items in whatever order they would like. This challenge can be done back to back, front to front, side to side, or however they can manage. Encourage them to take their time and to communicate with each other, as needed, to accomplish their goal.

As each set of partners is able to hold (without using hands) an item between them while standing together, remove the item so that they can hold the next item. The partners are to work until you call time. Have some way to celebrate and affirm their accomplishment of working together, perhaps by handing out candy or some other small favor.

Regroup, and debrief the experience:

- How difficult was it to accomplish this goal?
- If you were to do it alone, could you have succeeded?
- How important was it for your partner and you to communicate well?
- How did you work through any communication problems?

LOOK A LITTLE DEEPER (10–15 minutes)

Have a volunteer read aloud **1 Corinthians 13:4-7**. Then have another one read it, this time replacing the word *love* (and it's pronoun, *it*) with *friendship* (see page 39). Ask:

- What attitudes does the Scripture indicate that help us make and be friends?
- In addition to having these attitudes, what are some things people do to make and be friends? (*Showing interest in persons, finding out about their experiences and interests, listening to them, doing things together, working on a task together—things they have experienced in today's activities.*)

SENDING FORTH (2–5 minutes)

In a closing circle, lead your tweens in reading together **1 Corinthians 13:4-7,** replacing the word *love* (and it's pronoun, *it*) with the word *I*. (See page 39. Note that the verb changes to the first person singular.) After completing this, close your time together with a brief prayer.

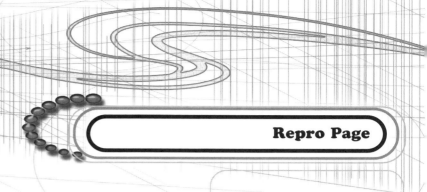

Friendship—
According to the Bible
1 Corinthians 13:4-7

Directions

Read and think about these adapted versions of the Scripture. The original word (instead of *friendship* or *I*) is *love* (and *it,* the pronoun referring to the word *love*).

- How well do these changes capture the meaning of the original?

<u>Friendship</u> is patient; <u>friendship</u> is kind;
<u>friendship</u> is not envious or boastful or arrogant or rude.
<u>Friendship</u> does not insist on its own way;
<u>friendship</u> is not irritable or resentful;
<u>friendship</u> does not rejoice in wrongdoing,
        but rejoices in the truth.
<u>Friendship</u> bears all things, believes all things,
        hopes all things, endures all things.

<u>I am</u> patient; <u>I am</u> kind;
<u>I am</u> not envious or boastful or arrogant or rude.
<u>I do</u> not insist on my own way;
<u>I am</u> not irritable or resentful;
<u>I do</u> not rejoice in wrongdoing,
        but <u>rejoice</u> in the truth.
<u>I bear</u> all things, <u>believe</u> all things,
<u>hope</u> all things, <u>endure</u> all things.

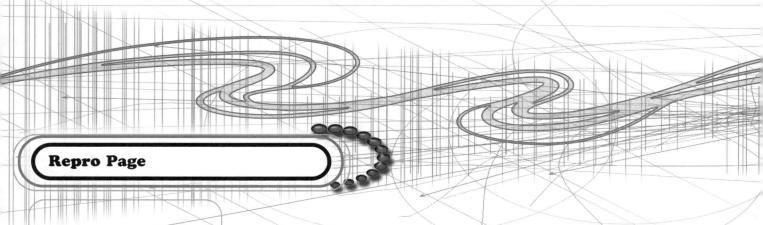

FAVORITE FACTS

Directions

Read over the list of subjects to the right. Use these subjects to find out more about the other members of your group. The blank at the bottom allows you to add an additional subject that you want to learn about a group member.

Talk one-on-one with a member of your group about one of the subjects. When you learn his or her answer, write it and the person's name in the space next to the subject.

This activity is not a timed competition; you can take some time to ask, "Why?" if you want to.

Favorite music
Favorite movie
Favorite sport
Favorite part of worship service
Favorite place outdoors
One thing I like about myself
Something that makes me happy
Something I'd like to try sometime
Something I wish
When I grow up, I
Something that makes me angry
If I were an animal, I would be

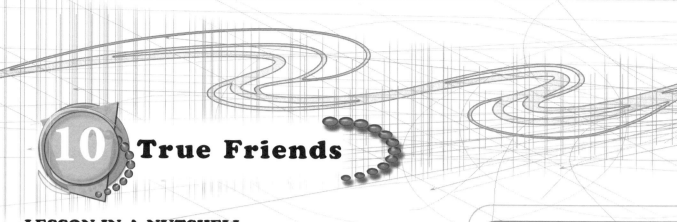

10 True Friends

LESSON IN A NUTSHELL

Friendships are wonderfully important to tweens. But friendships can also be very painful. This lesson helps tweens examine friendship and changes in friendships. It also reminds them that Jesus has called us friends and commanded us to love one another.

OUTLINING FRIENDSHIP (5–8 minutes)

As tweens arrive, direct them to pair up. Give each person a large sheet of paper cut from a roll of butcher paper. Have one partner lie down on the paper and the other draw an outline around him or her. Then have the pair switch duties. Do not put names with the outlines. Label one "A True Friend" and the other "A Not-So-True Friend." Remind the tweens that these labels are not descriptions of the person whose outline is there. The outline is just for the purpose of the activity.

A TRUE FRIEND OR NOT (10–15 minutes)

The tween partners are to work together to write words or phrases on the appropriate outline to describe what a true friend is and does and what a not-so-true friend is and does.

Give everyone a copy of the Scriptures (page 45). These proverbs can be a starting point for their task. But the tweens should also draw from their own life experiences for the descriptions. Completing this task will be richer if the pairs talk to each other about their ideas and experiences. Encourage them to do so.

After about six to eight minutes, give the tweens the repro page "Dear Diary" (page 44). Ask the pairs to read this scenario also and add to their descriptions on their outlines. Give the tweens a few more minutes to work as pairs.

After the allotted time, bring the tweens together to compare what they wrote. If you have a large number of tweens, have the pairs form small groups of four to six to go over the descriptions they wrote. You may want to include an adult, if possible.

Before They Arrive

❑ Make copies of repro pages 44–45 for each tween.

Supplies

❑ Bibles
❑ Large sheets of paper (A commercial size roll of butcher paper cut to lengths of six or seven feet will more than accommodate the heights of your tweens.)
❑ Index cards
❑ Pens or pencils
❑ Slips of paper or sticky notes
❑ Copies of the repro pages

Becoming a True Friend

FRIENDSHIPS CHANGE (10–12 minutes)

Ask the tweens whether their friends now are the same friends they had a year ago? three years ago? Also ask:

- Why do friendships change? (*interests change, families move away, school or classroom assignments change; individuals change*)
- How do you feel when you "lose a friend"?
- Is losing a friend your fault? (*Sometimes, if you have become a "not-so-true friend" and done such things as are on the list created earlier. Most likely not, if the circumstances change. The reasons may truly lie with the other person, and you have no control over what he or she thinks or does.*)
- What can you do to try to regain a friendship? (*You may need to ask for forgiveness or extend forgiveness in order to begin again.*)
- What can you do if it's clear you can't regain the friendship? (*Forgive the other person—and yourself—and do your best to go on without leaving each other with hard feelings; sometimes things just change.*)
- How do you make new friends? (*The list of what a true friend is and does will be a good starting point. Focus on some of those that are especially important for initiating a friendship.*)

A TRUE FRIEND FOREVER (5–7 minutes)

Introduce the tweens to **John 15:7-15.** Say: **Jesus was nearing the end of his life; he knew that the cross was ahead. He spoke these words to his disciples. They are words that remind us of God's love for each of us, of Jesus' love for his disciples—including us. And at the end, Jesus invites us to pass that love along to others.**

Close your eyes, relax. Imagine that you are one of Jesus' disciples. Which one will you be? Are you like Peter, bold and ready to get on with things? Are you like Thomas, a little uncertain about things? Are you like Matthew, coming from the experience of not being liked by others? Are you like Andrew, sort of in the shadow of your big brother Peter? Are you like Bartholomew, whom no one seems to notice much? Whoever you are, Jesus is speaking to you. Hear his words!

Read aloud **John 15:7-15.**

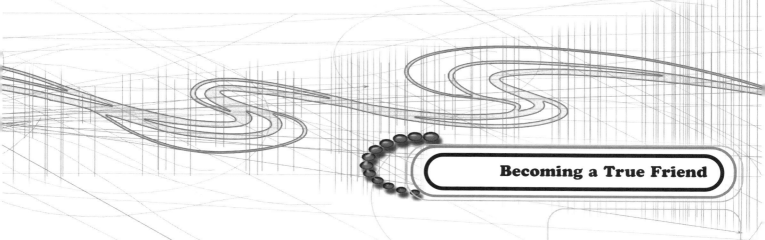

SENDING FORTH (3–5 minutes)

Have the tweens stay where they are, give them each a pencil and a small piece of paper (such as a sticky note). Invite them to think about what they have talked about today about friendship.

Refer them to their lists about a true friend and a not-so-true friend; recall their discussion about how friendships can change. Invite them to write on their paper the name of a friend whom they need to forgive in order to regain a friendship or to let go and move on. Ask them to pray silently about this friendship for a minute.

Then invite them to write the name of a person they know with whom they might begin a friendship. Remind them that a huge part of making a friend is to be the kind of friend you would want for yourself.

Encourage the tweens to take home their paper (or sticky note) with the name on it as reminder of their commitment to being a good friend.

Then close with this prayer:

Dear Jesus,

Thank you for loving us so much that you did indeed lay down your life for us. Thank you for showing us how to love one another. Help us be a true friend to you and to others. Amen.

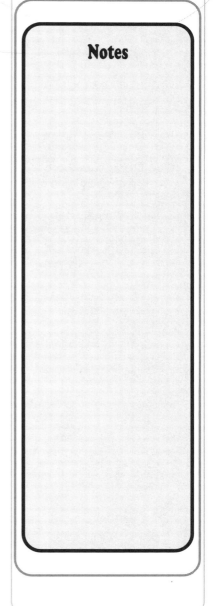

Notes

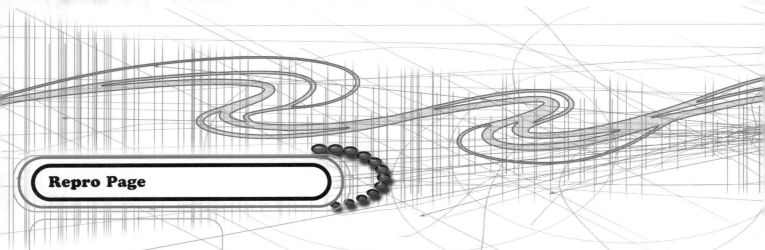

Dear Diary

Directions

Read this diary entry. What clues does it give you as to what a true friend is or does? about what a not-so-true friend is or does? Write your answers to these questions on your True Friend and Not-So-True Friend outlines.

Nobody loves me. I am just a worthless person. When I am at school, the "better than me" girls laugh at my hand-me-down clothes. These are nice clothes; both of my cousins wore them. They come from an expensive store.

My hair never looks right—always stringy and fly away—no matter what I do. I won't cut it short because one of my ears is bigger than the other. My grandmother says that I should be proud of my ears. One is a "Crockett" ear from my mom's family, and the other is a "Livingston" ear from my dad's family. How can I be proud of something that people laugh at me about?

Every day just gets worse. I live on a farm and ride the bus to school. Popular kids have parents or maids to take them to school. My mom is mentally ill. She takes medicine, but the voices in her head cause her to talk out loud to people no one else can see. Everyone knows about my mom. Some people say that I will grow up to be just like her. They tease me and run away from me.

Except for Susan. Susan is nice to me. We eat lunch together, and she has even ridden the bus home with me. Susan is my best friend. I can talk to her about anything—even about my mom.

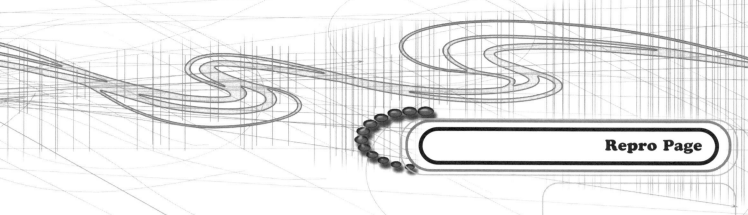

Friends—
According to God's Word

Directions

Read these Scriptures from the Book of Proverbs.

What clues do they give you as to what a true friend is or does? about what a not-so-true friend is or does? Write these on your outlines.

Gossip is no good! It causes hard feelings and comes between friends. (Proverbs 16:28, CEV)

You will keep your friends if you forgive them, but you will lose your friends if you keep talking about what they did wrong. (Proverbs 17:9, CEV)

The start of an argument is like a water leak—so stop it before real trouble breaks out. (Proverbs 17:14, CEV)

A friend is always a friend. (Proverbs 17:17a, CEV)

Some friends don't help, but a true friend is closer than your own family. (Proverbs 18:24, CEV)

The rich have many friends; the poor have none. . . . Everyone tries to be friends of those who can help them. If you are poor, your own relatives reject you, and your friends are worse. When you really need them, they are not there. (Proverbs 19:4a-7, CEV)

What matters most is loyalty. It's better to be poor than to be a liar. Showing respect to the LORD brings true life. (Proverbs 19:22-23a, CEV)

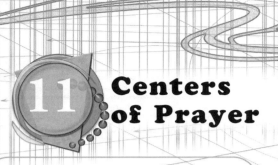

11 Centers of Prayer

Before They Arrive

❑ Choose how you will present the Lord's Prayer. If your church library has *The Visual Bible: Matthew* on VHS or DVD, you may choose to use the segment with the Lord's Prayer.
❑ Gather supplies and set up the Lord's Prayer centers, including the posters with the instructions.
❑ Have copies of the Prayer is... ranking activity available for each tween.

Supplies

❑ Bibles
❑ Supplies for the individual centers (listed with the center information)
❑ Posterboard and markers

Note

This session plan uses the basic wording for the Lord's Prayer, as found in Matthew 6:5-15 (NRSV). You may choose to use the traditional wording if your tweens are more familiar with that as part of your church's liturgy.

LESSON IN A NUTSHELL

Most tweens, even those who have not been active in church, are familiar with the Lord's Prayer. But have they ever thought about what the prayer means to them? Centers of Prayer offers a variety of activities designed to draw deeper meaning from a familiar prayer.

PRAYER IS . . . (5–10 minutes)

As tweens arrive, have them complete the Prayer Is . . . ranking activity and My Thoughts on Prayer (page 49). After all of the tweens have arrived, invite them to talk about their responses to the activities.

PRAY LIKE THIS (3–5 minutes)

Say: **Through prayer we grow closer in our relationship with God. Jesus provided a model for prayer.**

Choose from these options to present the Lord's Prayer to the tweens:

- Show the Matthew video, cued to Matthew 6:5-15.
- Have an actor dressed in costume portray Jesus and act out the story of Matthew 6:5-15.
- Read the text.

Say: **Today we will be experiencing the Lord's Prayer in a variety of different ways.**

LORD'S PRAYER CENTERS (30–45 minutes)

Direct the tweens to work in groups of two or three to experience the various centers. Allow the tweens to move from center to center as they finish each one; encourage them to spend as much time as needed in each place. Have them leave their creations at the center.

Drawing Center

"Our Father in heaven, hallowed be your name."

Supplies: Art paper, pencils, crayons, markers, paints and brushes, other drawing media, a dictionary

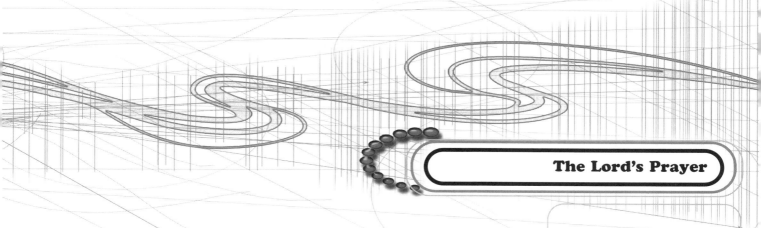

Poster: What does it mean to call God "Father"? What does "hallowed" mean? Draw or paint your response to one or both of these questions.

Torn-Paper Collage

"Your kingdom come. Your will be done, on earth as it is in heaven."

Supplies: Construction paper in a variety of colors, patterned craft paper, wallpaper samples, various other types of paper, glue

Poster: God's will—to ask for it is to expect it. What does God's will look like? What would earth under God's will look like? Tear paper into shapes and glue them onto paper to form an image. Your torn-paper collage is to show how you imagine your world would be if God's will were done on earth.

Pipe Cleaner Center

"Give us this day our daily bread."

Supplies: Chenille stems or pipe cleaners

Poster: What do you need to live every day? What can you survive without? Think about the things God provides in your daily life. Using the pipe cleaners, form an image of the "daily bread" that God provides in your life every day for which you are most thankful.

Prayer Beads

"And forgive us our debts, as we also forgive our debtors."

Supplies: "Pony" craft beads, plastic or leather lacing in 16 inch lengths, slip rings (available at craft stores or discount stores)

Poster: Every day we sin against others, and others sin against us. When we pray, we ask God to forgive our sins against others in the same way that we have forgiven those who have sinned against us. Make prayer beads. Use these beads to pray for those whom you have sinned against in thought, word, and action. Ask God for forgiveness. Offer forgiveness to those who have sinned against you.

Special Tips

Feel free to use other media in a center as an alternative to those suggested here.

Prayer Bead Instructions

Take a 16" piece of lacing. Fold in half. Attach the lacing to the slip ring with a loop knot by pulling the two loose ends through the loop end of the lacing as it wraps around the ring. Slip one bead for each prayer onto one of the strips of lacing.

Tie a knot at the end of each row of beads. Attach the slip ring to your key ring or backpack as a reminder to offer daily prayers of forgiveness.

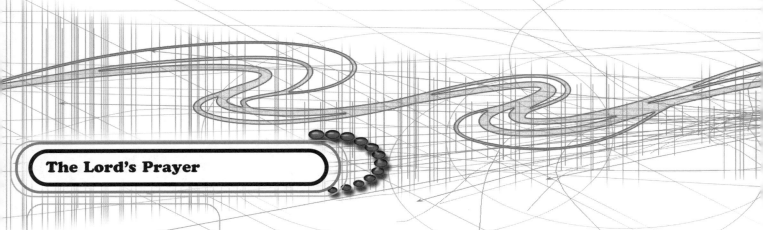

The Lord's Prayer

The Labyrinth

The labyrinth is found in different forms in cultures throughout the world. The oldest known Christian labyrinth dates from 328. Early Christians used the labyrinth as a symbolic pilgrimage to Jerusalem. During the time of the Crusades, pilgrimages to the Holy Land were both dangerous and expensive. By walking the labyrinth, these Christians simulated the spiritual journey of the pilgrimage to Jerusalem.

For more information on the labyrinth, go to: www.labyrinths.org.

A labyrinth should not be confused with a maze. A maze contains dead ends. A labyrinth is a circular or winding path that leads into and out of a center space. The act of walking the labyrinth is an individual experience. Christians today still use the labyrinth as a means of connecting with God.

Labyrinth Center

"And do not bring us to the time of trial, but rescue us from the evil one."

Supplies: Copies of the finger labyrinth (on page 49), quiet music CD

Poster: Temptation, or "the time of trial," exists in many forms. As you listen to the music and walk the labyrinth, consider the ways in which you are tempted. What draws you into temptation? Walk the labyrinth. Stop along the way to seek God's guidance for ways to overcome temptation.

Litany Center

"For yours is the kingdom and the power and the glory forever and ever. Amen."

Supplies: paper, pencil

Poster: Through prayer, we express our concerns and thanksgivings to God. Write a litany of praise to God, expressing God's kingdom, power, and glory forever and ever. Leave the litany here to be added to by others.

SENDING FORTH (5–10 minutes)

Gather the tweens at the first center. Move from center to center as you pray.

Say: **As we pray the prayer Jesus gave us, we will take time to share what we created and experienced at our centers today.**

Our Father in heaven, hallowed be your name. (*Take time for sharing.*)

Your kingdom come. Your will be done, on earth as it is in heaven. (*Take time for sharing.*)

Give us this day our daily bread. (*Take time for sharing.*)

And forgive us our debts, as we also have forgiven our debtors. (*Take time for sharing.*)

And do not bring us to the time of trial, but rescue us from the evil one. (*Take time for sharing.*)

For yours is the kingdom and the power and the glory forever and ever. Amen. (*Read the litanies.*)

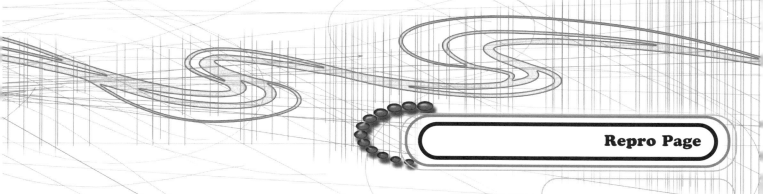

Prayer Is . . .

Important in my life	I'm not sure	Agree	Disagree
Something I do every day	I'm not sure	Agree	Disagree
Talking to God	I'm not sure	Agree	Disagree
Worthwhile	I'm not sure	Agree	Disagree
Listening to God	I'm not sure	Agree	Disagree

My Thoughts on Prayer

Use the back of this paper to write your thoughts on prayer. Use the questions in the right margin if they are helpful to you. Save this paper for later.

The Labyrinth

The labyrinth used in this lesson is modeled after the labyrinth in the Chartres Cathedral in Chartres, France. The labyrinth in Chartres has been used since the time of the Crusades.

Directions

Do you agree or disagree with these statements about what prayer is? Circle your answer.

Then in your own words, write what you think about prayer. You may use these questions to start your thinking:

- What does prayer mean to you?
- Why do you pray?
- Where do you pray?
- For what or whom do you pray?

Labyrinth Instructions

Walk the labyrinth by tracing the path with your finger or with a pencil or crayon. You may color the path as you "walk."

- As you move to the center, consider the ways you are tempted.
- When you arrive at the center, spend time with God seeking guidance for ways in which to overcome temptation.
- As you walk out of the labyrinth, thank God for the strength to overcome temptation.

12 Party On!

Before They Arrive

❑ Review this session throughout the year and plan for its success.

Supplies

❑ Copies of page 58, the Scripture for the day
❑ Supplies needed for the games
❑ Ingredients needed for any food the will be made or assembled by the tweens
❑ Decorations
❑ Plates, cups, utensils for eating and serving, napkins, serving bowls and platters
❑ Posterboard, marker

LESSON IN A NUTSHELL

The tweens will organize a party to celebrate God's love and goodness and to welcome next year's tweens into their fellowship group. The elder tweens will have functioned as Secret Tween Buddies to the new tweens, and the identities will be revealed at the party.

Planning Required!

THROUGHOUT-THE-YEAR PLANNING

For this party to be a fun-filled and memorable one at year's end, planning must start early. One approach is to allot some time at the end of each meeting (or most meetings) for current tweens to talk about how they might celebrate God's love in the form of a party for new tweens. Tween leaders should feel free to offer suggestions as well.

The ideas garnered from these planning sessions should be written down on a posterboard. Each time they meet, the tweens may review their list and add new ideas. As the time for the party draws near, the tweens should review all the ideas and select ones they want to carry out. The tweens need to establish a theme, come up with decoration and food ideas, and gather game ideas. (Some suggestions are on pages 54–57, and 59.)

Deal also with budget issues. Will you need to do some fundraising? (Car washes, bake sales, pet walking, pet sitting are appropriate for this age group.) You may want to e-mail (or snail mail) the list of ideas and materials to the tweens, their parents, and leaders as a way of continuing to refine the plans and delegate responsibilities.

Establish a time table for your planning. Set deadlines for the various steps, including sending invitations and securing party materials. Help the tweens take responsibility. Part of what you are doing in this experience is teaching young persons how to plan and how to take on and follow through with responsibility. These are important life skills.

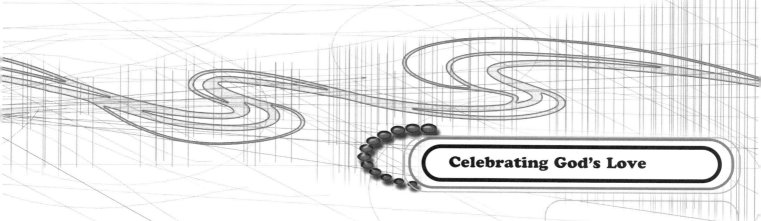

SET UP SECRET TWEEN BUDDIES

About two months before the party, set up your Secret Tween Buddies program. Begin by talking with your tweens about the fact that each person is special in God's eyes and that we are learning to look at others with "God's eyes." Talk about how each of us enjoys being made to feel special. It feels good when someone notices us in a positive way. Point out that mysteries are fun too. Come up with a list of ways to be a Secret Tween Buddy. Here is a general plan for this program; feel free to modify it:

- With the help of the tweens, the church office, Sunday school teachers, come up with a list of persons who will be eligible for your tween program next year. (See Special Tip also.) Develop as much information about each future tween as possible, including such things as address, school, hobbies, likes and dislikes, and so forth. You may want to design a questionnaire to be filled out by next year's tweens to gather more information. (You may want your current tweens to fill out the same questionnaire so that you can more easily create pairs.)

- Use the information you have to pair each current tween with a future tween. The tweens will secretly send notes, do nice things, and give small gifts to their secret buddies over the designated time. They will need to be clever so as not to be discovered. The grand revealing will occur at the party.

- When you make assignments, be sure to establish boundaries. For example, each week a tween must do something for the secret buddy; tweens may spend no more than an average of one (maybe, two) dollars a week (you determine the amount). Remind the tweens that they can be creative in their thoughtfulness; being kind doesn't mean spending lots of money.

- Set aside time at each tween meeting to have the tweens talk about what they have done for their secret buddy that week. The ideas of one tween may spark the imagination and energy of the others.

- Have the tweens plan for one special party favor for their particular Buddy, something that they think will be just right for the person they are paired with. You may want to set a special dollar value for this also. Or you may want to go to a local Christian bookstore and purchase a variety of small items for the tweens to give to their buddy. Or if you have a special name for your tween fellowship group, you may want to create a t-shirt or other customized item to show the new tweens that they are welcomed into the group. (Cokesbury Specialty Imprints is one source of custom-designed t-shirts; call 1-800-237-7511 for information.)

Special Tip

Encourage your tweens to think also of potential tweens who are not in the church. The attention paid to the secret buddy may be just what he or she needs to make a decision to come to church—at least to the Tween Time fellowship.

Special Tips

Be sure to clear with the church office or staff well in advance the time and location for the party.

As the adult leader, you and your adult team may want to call each parent. This personal contact will generate more support and allow parents to ask any questions they may have. Time spent on the phone will pay dividends for the party and for next year's meetings.

CREATE AND SEND INVITATIONS

As part of your ongoing planning, the tweens will have developed a theme and, perhaps, a look. You may want to use original tween art for the invitation and/or use software to design the invitations for the party.

Send the invitation via regular mail, but plan a campaign to ensure that the future tweens come. Send an e-mail reminder, make phone calls, put reminders in the church bulletin and newsletter; make an announcement in worship service.

The mailed invitations need to include a permission slip for parents or guardians and their tween to sign. The slip should also specify how partygoers will be getting to and from the party.

The Day of the Party

LET'S GET READY (30–60 minutes)

Have your tween group come early to help set up for the party. Divide them into pairs or teams and give them instructions based on the activities the tweens have chosen. Encourage them to work quickly. When they have their tasks completed, have them ask for an adult leader to go over their checklist to make sure that everything is ready.

WELCOME THE NEW TWEENS (10 minutes)

Designate tweens to be greeters to welcome the guests to the party. They may give out nametags and photograph the newcomers, using a digital or instant camera. All of the current tweens and leaders need to wear nametags as well. Part of welcoming people is to make them comfortable in the new group. Knowing the names of the others there is helpful to newcomers.

You can use the photographs from the celebration in a variety of ways:

- Post them on a bulletin board and then add them to your tween group scrapbook.
- Use a software program or copy shop to make a calendar for next year, with the photos from the party and the dates of the meetings. Give a calendar to each tween.

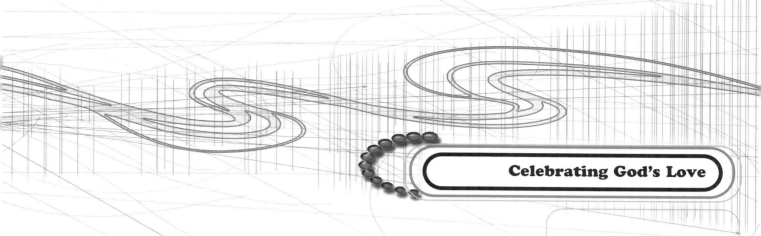

GAME TIME (30–40 minutes)

Play various games that your tweens have planned. Check out the Obstacle Challenge Course on page 59 as one possibility for group building. Additional games are on pages 54–55.

MEET AND EAT (20–25 minutes)

Now is the time the new tweens find out who their Secret Tween Buddy is. Make a big production of this. Drum roll, "Oscar" envelope suspense, guessing games—these are some fun ways to add to the announcement.

When everyone knows his or her buddy, the buddies are to sit together at the table and enjoy the refreshments (see pages 56–57 for ideas). The elder tweens give a party favor to their Secret Buddy. The elder tweens use the gift to talk with the new tween about what the group has done and what being part of the tweens fellowship has meant to them. This conversation is a way of reinforcing the invitation for the new tween to participate also. The tweens can also have fun telling tales of what they had to do to keep the younger one from finding out the identity of their buddy.

CLEAN-UP TIME (5 minutes)

The tweens and their guests will engage in a quick clean-up of the party space. One person (preferably a tween) will brief everyone as to where garbage goes and where any non-disposables and recyclables belong. Then he or she can announce that when they hear the music play, everyone is to clean fast and furiously. When the music stops, everyone is to stop and look for more areas to clean when the music starts again. Use the music until all is cleaned up. Congratulate the tweens for working so well together.

SENDING FORTH (5–7 minutes)

Bring the group together for a closing circle.

Say: **Today we had a great time of fellowship. As Christians, we recognize that the source of joy in our lives is God; we are celebrating God's love and seeing that love in one another**.

Give the tweens a copy of page 58, which is the Scripture for the day. Divide them into two groups and have them read it aloud.

Close with prayer or your tweens' special ritual.

Special Tips

Coach your tweens in advance as to how to make sure that all of the new tweens are included in the games.

Take more photographs during the games and clean up. Be sure to take photos of the Secret Tween Buddies too.

After-Party To-Do:

Have the tweens write thank-you notes to all of the people who helped them make the party a reality, including the chaperones and the future tweens.

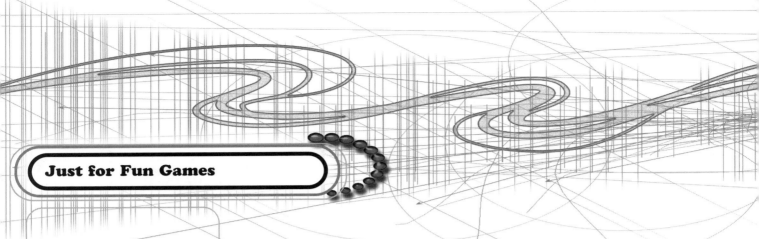

Notes

BIBLE TIMES DRESS-UP RELAY

Gather two or more piles of "Bible times' clothing depending upon how large a gathering you will have. Bathrobes are good for this; take the belt off the bathrobe, and put it in the pile. In the pile also put a cloth for the "headdress" and an old necktie or piece of rope or twine to tie around the headdress to secure it. Add a walking stick (or a yardstick) for a staff. Add a pair of sandals or flip flops. .

Divide the tweens into equal groups. The groups will race one person at a time to put on the Bible times clothing (tying the belt, securing the headdress, and picking up the staff and tapping it three times on the floor). Then that person takes off the clothes, leaving them in a pile again and races to tag the next member of the team who then has to dress as a Bible times person and undress again.

First team with everyone managing to dress as a Bible times person and then discard the clothing wins.

PILE OF SHOES

Do this relay on a surface inside and make sure that it is clean and free of sharp objects.

Ask everyone to take off their shoes. Throw all right shoes in one large pile at one end of the room. Pile all the left shoes in another large pile at the other end of the room.

Divide the group into two teams.

Designate one team to start with the pile of right shoes and one team to start with the pile of left shoes. At your signal the first person on a team will run to their pile find their shoe, put it on, run back and tag the next person. Once everyone on a team has on one shoe, they go through the process again, this time running for their other shoe. The team with everyone wearing both shoes wins.

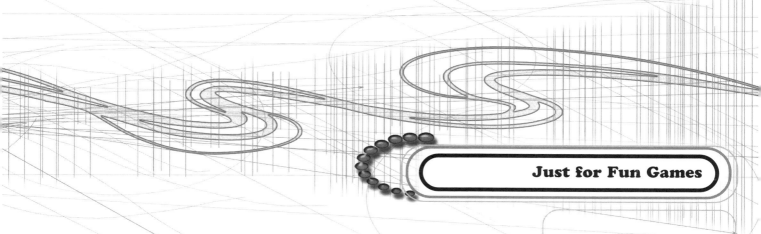

BACKWARDS

Have a relay race that requires absolutely no props.

Divide the group into a manageable number of tweens per team. Designate a starting point and an ending point. As each new player is tagged, he or she must go from start to finish backwards, then turn around and run back to tag the next member of the team.

For each team member shout out a different instruction. Some suggestions, walking backward, running backward, skipping backward, hopping backward, and crawling backward.

For a variation, each team member may decide upon how they are going to get from start to finish—as long as they do it BACKWARD!

SQUAT TAG

To be safe in this version of tag, players must squat.

Mark an area of play; or if playing outdoors, designate boundaries of the play area. Everyone must stay inside this area while playing the game. Anyone who leaves the area is automatically out of the game.

"It" may tag any player who is standing up. Tagged players join "It" to tag other players. Players are only safe when squatting.

Players are NOT allowed to squat during the entire game. They must use part of their time trying to evade "It" and those who have already been tagged.

ATLANTA BANANA

In order to fully participate, players need to discover the catch or right combination of items to be allowed to go along on this venture. The leader begins by saying, "I'm going to Atlanta to buy bananas. Where are you going?"

To answer correctly, the next player must name a city and a fruit. (Do not let the players know that the fruit must start with a letter that follows the letter that begins the name of the city. For example, "I'm going to **N**ewport to buy **o**ranges.) If the player answers incorrectly, say, "No, you may not go." If the player answers correctly, say, "Yes, you may go." In either case, say to the next player, "I'm going to Atlanta to buy bananas" and see whether he or she can answer correctly. Play continues until everyone has figured out the trick or until interest wanes.

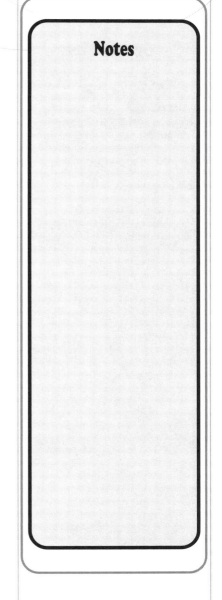

Notes

MAKE SPECIAL-ORDER SUNDAES

You will need bowls and spoons, vanilla ice cream (and additional flavors if you wish), several kinds of toppings, nuts (be very careful not to use peanuts if anyone in your group has a peanut allergy). Optional: Have on hand bananas to make banana splits.

Divide your tweens into pairs. You might use this activity to introduce your Secret Tween Buddies or just to have them do something special together.

Each person in a pair is to make a sundae for the other person, and the tweens MUST make the sundae exactly as the person they are making it for instructs them to. Each person in the pair will be both the maker of a sundae and the receiver of a sundae.

After the sundaes are made have the group come back to a general area and enjoy their sundaes.

You might want them to then discuss how it felt to give the instructions and to follow someone else's instructions.

POTATO BAR

You will need a cookie sheet; a knife; bowls or plates and spoons for use with the toppings; bowls, spoons, and forks for eating the potatoes; large, uniform-size baking potatoes; toppings such as plain yogurt, shredded or melted cheddar cheese, shredded Swiss cheese, taco sauce or salsa, butter or margarine, salt and pepper, diced bell pepper, chopped chives, bacon bits, raw or steamed broccoli.

Scrub the potatoes with a vegetable brush under running water. Dry the potatoes, pierce the skin, place them on a cookie sheet, and bake them at 425 degrees for one hour.

While the potatoes bake, prepare any toppings that need to be chopped, sliced, or cooked. Then set out the toppings on a long table, with access to both sides.

Carefully slice each potato in half lengthwise before serving so that each participant may have one half potato.

Allow the participants to choose from the toppings offered. Caution everyone that the freshly baked potatoes are very hot.

Special Tips

The potatoes may be baked ahead of time and reheated, or they may be baked just before the party is to start.

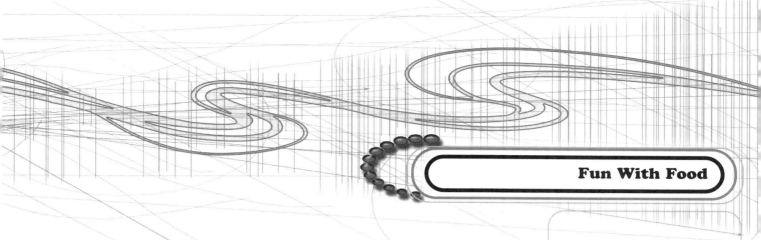

COLD FRUIT SOUP

Have on hand a blender; a spatula; cups or bowls; spoons; 4 cups ripe fresh or frozen* berries or peaches, cleaned and cut up; 2 cups vanilla yogurt; 2 cups low-fat milk; honey or sugar to taste.

In a blender, process together two parts fruit, one part yogurt, and one part milk. Sweeten to taste with honey or sugar. Chill before serving. Yields about 8 one-cup servings.

*To eat this soup immediately after preparing it, use frozen fruit and very cold yogurt and milk.

S'MORES

Have on hand a microwave oven or standard oven, paper towels if using a microwave oven or cookie sheets if using a standard oven, plates, graham crackers, chocolate candy bars, and marshmallows.

Standard Oven Method: For each S'more, have the tweens top one graham cracker with some of the chocolate bar, a marshmallow, and a second cracker and press them together. Bake at 350 degrees for 2 minutes.

Microwave Oven Method: For each S'more, have the tweens top one cracker with chocolate and a marshmallow. Place on a microwaveable plate or a paper towel and microwave on high for 10 to 15 seconds or until the marshmallow is softened. Cover with a second cracker and press together slightly.

Be sure to warn the tweens that the S'more, especially the marshmallow part, will be hot.

ROLL-UPS

Have on hand plates; forks, knives, and spoons for applying sandwich ingredients; flour tortillas; sandwich meats; cheeses; chopped and sliced fruits and vegetables suitable for sandwiches; peanut butter; salad dressings; and condiments.

Set out the ingredients on a long table, with access to both sides of the table. Let tweens assemble their own sandwiches by applying the ingredients of their choice to a tortilla and then rolling up the tortilla with the ingredients inside.

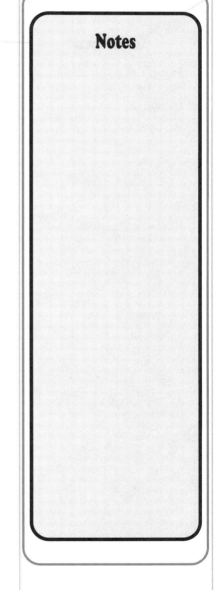

Notes

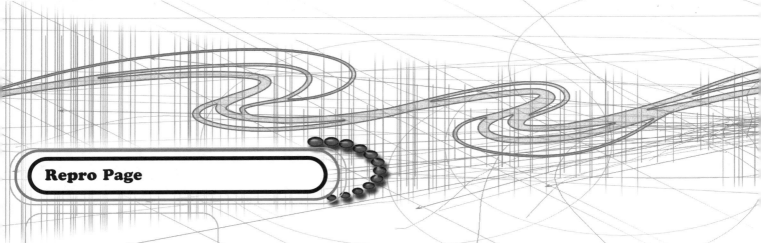

Celebrating God's Love
A Litany of Philippians 4:4-7a (CEV)

Directions

In two groups, read aloud this Scripture for today.

Group 1: Always be glad because of the Lord!

Group 2: I will say it again: Be glad.

Group 1: Always be gentle with others.

Group 2: The Lord will soon be here.

Group 1: Don't worry about anything,

Group 2: but pray about everything.

Group 1: With thankful hearts

Group 2: offer up your prayers and requests to God.

Group 1: Then, because you belong to Christ Jesus,

Group 2: God will bless you with peace.

All: Amen!

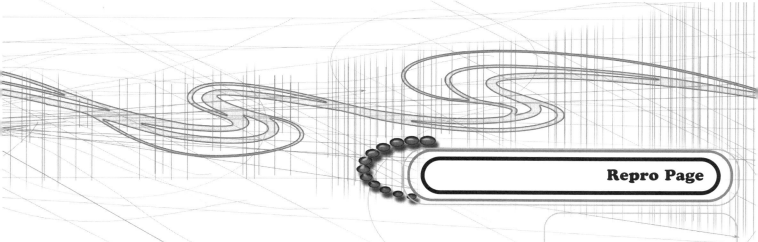

OBSTACLE CHALLENGE COURSE

Focus: Caring for one another.

Scripture: Ecclesiastes 4:9-10a ("Two are better than one... For if they fall, one will lift up the other.")

Space: A large area, either indoors or outside

Supplies: Lengths of rope or string, bungee chords, miscellaneous objects, blindfolds

Preparation: Create a three-dimensional obstacle course. Use rope and bungee cords strung across the area at various angles. Attach them to trees, chairs, door knobs, or other sturdy holders. Scatter the objects on the floor, or if possible, hang down a few lightweight ones from the overhead ropes.

The First Challenge: Successfully lead your partner through the obstacle course without touching any of the objects or other people in the course.

Pair a current tween with a new one. The new one is blindfolded. The current tween is to lead the the blindfolded one through the challenge course with voice only! If the blindfolded person touches an object or another person, the pair has to count out loud to 77 (by ones) before moving forward.

When the pair has gotten through the course, the new tween becomes the leader and the current tween is blindfolded. They go back through the course, starting where they ended previously.

The Second Challenge: This time partners must tie a blindfold around their ankles and do the course three-legged.

Debriefing: After time is up or all have finished the course, sit together and respond to these questions. Invite more than one person to answer each.

- What was it like to be blindfolded and led? How did you feel?
- What was it like to be the guide? What did you do to be helpful?
- What was it like to go through the course three-legged?
- How does this experience relate to the Scripture (Ecclesiastes 4:9-10a)?
- How can we as Christians help one another in our tween group?

Directions

Copy this page and give it to a team of tweens and adults to set up the course and give the directions for the challenges. Be sure to make time for the debriefing.

Quiz

Can you guess why this challenge uses the count of 77? Hint: The answer comes from Scripture.

Service Programs

1 Mission Starts at Home

LESSON IN A NUTSHELL

This lesson is designed to help your group by providing a safe "mission field" in which to start their Christian practice of service to others. It will also help the parents appreciate the kind of effort their preteens are capable of when they embrace tasks for themselves.

DISCOVERING THE NEED

Oftentimes, "mission work" is equated with helping people some place else, often in an exotic location. The idea of mission work can be daunting, especially to young people who haven't spent much time away from home. Conversely, parents often bemoan the absence of their sons and daughters, who seem willing to accomplish great tasks everywhere but at home.

GETTING READY

❑ Gather supplies, including potpourri and baskets or other containers.
❑ Send notes to parents explaining this project. Tell the parents that their tweens are offering extra service at home as an act of love to their families and as an act of faith in God.

GATHER 'N' GAB (10–15 minutes)

As the tweens arrive, direct them to the large sheets of paper and markers. Have them write or draw pictures of various projects at home they have attempted with their families. Or they may indicate the chores for which they are responsible around their homes.

Invite them to tell the stories behind their words or drawings. Ask:

▪ Is it harder or easier to do a project for your family than for someone else? Why?

GOD'S WORD (7–10 minutes)

Invite different persons to read **Exodus 20:1-18,** focusing on verse 12.

Say: **When the Hebrew people left Egypt, they found themselves free for the first time in anyone's memory. God gave them the Ten Commandments to help them identify themselves as God's people and to help them live with one**

Supplies

❑ Bibles
❑ Large sheets of paper
❑ Markers
❑ Potpourri
❑ Baskets or other simple containers
❑ Ribbons and scissors
❑ Paper of various colors
❑ Pens

Something to Consider

How well do you know the family situations of your tweens? Are any living in single-parent households, with blended families, with grandparents, in foster care? Take care in your use of language in this program to be inclusive of the many types of families your tweens may represent.

- Why do you suppose that is a commandment?
- What difference does it make in a family whether persons honor their parents?

TWEENS IN MISSION (20–25 minutes)

Explain to the tweens that they are offering service at home as an act of love to their parents and as an act of faith in God. These are not "chores" that are required of them. They are extra tasks meant to be special acts of love. Their service to their families is a way of pleasing God and being in mission.

Ask the tweens, as a group, to come up with a list of household projects they could do to help their families. Some examples include trim trees, mow grass, vacuum rugs and carpets, dust furniture, prepare dinner, and so forth. Then have each tween choose at least two projects or tasks to do at home.

Spread the baskets and containers out on the table. Have the tweens fill them with potpourri and write a note to their parents, telling them that they will be honoring them through their service and indicating what projects they have committed to do. Have the tweens decorate the containers with ribbon and attach the note. The tweens will take these home to give to their parents.

SNACK 'N' YACK (20 minutes)

Serve refreshments and talk about the experience. Ask:

- What is the hardest part about working at home?
- Do you think that your project will be different from what you normally do around your home?
- How can your home be your mission field?

SENDING FORTH (5–8 minutes)

Have everyone form a circle. Invite the group to pray for their families, either aloud or silently. Then close with this prayer:

God, we know you want us to honor our parents. We do not always want to, but we know that honoring them is pleasing to you. Help us be the sons and daughters you want us to be. Be with our parents also. We pray for blessings upon our families; increase the love we have for one another. Amen.

Special Tips

Make time during the week to call or e-mail the tweens to ask how their parents responded. That's a gentle way of reminding the tweens to follow through if they have not yet done so.

In your next meeting, invite tweens to talk about the experience of being in mission at home. Thank them for their great start to developing the Christian practice of serving others.

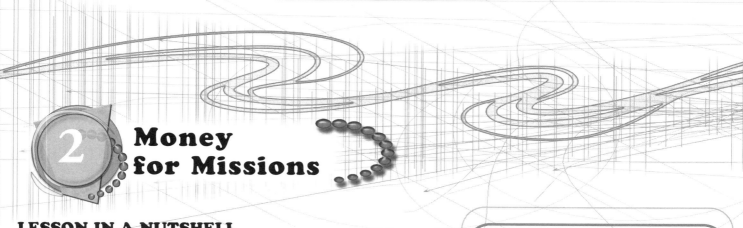

2 Money for Missions

LESSON IN A NUTSHELL

Your tweens will learn about a Christian ministry in your community and decide how to conduct a fundraising campaign in the congregation to support the ministry. By developing this short-term partnership, your tweens will be helping Christ "in preaching good news to the poor, proclaiming freedom for the prisoners and recovery of sight for the blind, and releasing the oppressed."

DISCOVERING THE NEED

Your church denomination, local chamber of commerce, charitable funding agency, ministerial alliance, or phone book should be able to direct you to reputable Christian ministries in your area. Involve your tweens in selecting a worthy group to support.

GETTING READY

❏ Gain support from your pastor, finance committee, and any other groups who need to endorse this project. Some churches have guidelines regarding fundraising and/or the solicitation of money.
❏ Contact the ministry provider. Schedule a day and time when your group can visit and take a tour of their facility. Ask whether there are any special instructions for the visiting tweens.
❏ Distribute medical/liability release or other permission forms.
❏ Arrange for enough drivers and chaperones.
❏ Have the tweens bring a few dollars to cover the cost of pizzas. Call ahead, and have your local pizza shop deliver pizzas and drinks. Cheese and pepperoni pizzas seem to be favorites among this age group.

GATHER 'N' GAB (10 minutes)

As the tweens arrive, collect the permissions slips and make assignments to vehicles. Tell the group a little about the ministry you will be visiting. Be sure to indicate any special instructions the tweens are to observe in their visit.

Supplies

❏ Bibles
❏ Permission forms
❏ Camera (a disposable one will make it easier for tweens to do the photographing)
❏ Large sheets of paper and markers

Look Ahead

Review the project, and schedule the fundraising campaign and the trip (either before or after the fundraising) to suit your time frame.

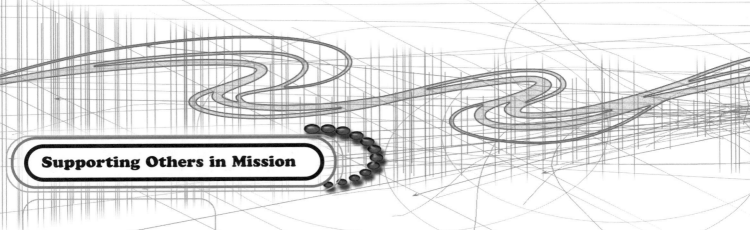

Supporting Others in Mission

Special Tips

Visiting the ministry organization *after* collecting money is alternative plan. If you go then, the tweens may hand deliver the check for the ministry.

If your group delivers the funds they have raised, here is a prayer for the occasion:

O God, as we deliver this gift to _____, may we realize that we are helping them fulfill your mission on earth—preaching to the poor, proclaiming freedom to the prisoners, recovering the sight of the blind, and releasing those who are oppressed. Amen.

GOD'S WORD (8–15 minutes)

Make a list on a large sheet of paper of what the tweens say Jesus' purpose was. Have a volunteer read aloud **Luke 4:18** from a modern translation. Make connections between what the tweens stated and the Scripture.

As far as Jesus was concerned, he was sent to:

- preach good news to the poor
- proclaim freedom for the prisoners
- recover the sight of the blind
- release the oppressed

Ask:

- What does it mean to be oppressed? (*Definition: To be held down, crushed, or burdened by someone or something*)
- In it what ways are people oppressed today? (*Some examples: poverty, drugs, hunger, lack of education or opportunity, lack of hope, and so on*)
- How do you think _____ (the ministry you are assisting) helps Jesus preach to the poor, proclaim freedom to the prisoners, recover the sight of the blind, and/or release the oppressed?

Point out that the tweens will be helping the chosen ministry achieve this goal by providing money for their work. Give the tweens a few minutes to talk about the joy of helping this ministry fulfill Christ's mission.

TWEENS IN MISSION (60–90 minutes)

Encourage your tweens to listen attentively and ask good questions. A few questions are listed below:

- How did this ministry get started?
- What services do you provide to the community?
- How do you help Jesus preach to the poor, proclaim freedom to the prisoners, recover the sight of the blind, and/or release those who are oppressed?
- What is the ministry's greatest need?
- Are there specific items for which we could raise money to support your ministry?
- Are there other ways we can help you in the future?

If you have permission, have the tweens take photographs that they may use later in their publicity. Or ask the organization for flyers the tweens may use.

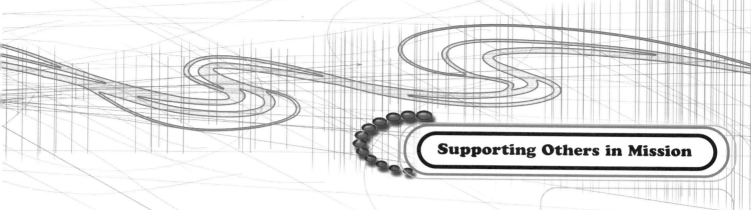

SNACK 'N' YACK (25–35 minutes)

Upon returning to the church, serve pizzas and drinks (order them before leaving the ministry site). Talk about the experience:

- What did you see or experience today for the first time?
- What aspect of their ministry most impressed you?
- What's one thing you will remember about today's experience?
- Are you interested in assisting them in the future? If yes, how?

Together, plan your fundraising campaign. The group will need to

❑ Publicize the need and the campaign. Suggest such things as a slogan the tweens come up with, special announcements made by volunteer tweens, information written by tweens for the church newsletter or bulletin, posters and flyers designed by tweens, special envelopes or collection receptacles decorated by the tweens. Have the tweens make a list and assignments.

❑ Decide whether the fundraising will be a special one-day emphasis, a seasonal or short-term emphasis, a contest between groups within the church, or an ongoing project.

❑ Set a timeline for getting things done: creating the publicity, beginning and ending the campaign, and delivering or sending the check.

❑ Choose whether to collect pennies, spare change, dollar bills, or just whatever people want to give.

❑ Determine whether the money will be collected in large plastic jugs or boxes, the collection plates, special envelopes, or another method befitting of your congregation. Some churches, for instance, may ask people to bring their gift to the altar.

❑ Double check to see that everyone has a role in making the campaign work. If tweens want to work in small groups, encourage that. Discuss the agreed upon time and assignments once again for clarity.

SENDING FORTH (2–3 minutes)

With the plan agreed upon, join in a closing circle. Briefly review the highlights of the experience, especially in light of the Scripture. Point out that by joining together, Christians are able to do more ministry than if each person were on his or her own.

Pray: **Dear God, please continue to bless _____ (ministry name) and the good things they are doing for you. May they—and we—be faithful in fulfilling your mission on earth. Amen.**

Special Tips

Churches often have detailed money-handling procedures. Be sure to know and follow them.

Don't be offended if you or your tweens are not allowed to handle the money. Your church money-handling policies are designed for protection.

The financial secretary will need to cut a final check for you to hand deliver or send to the ministry.

When Time Matters

If you have additional time, follow up the planning of the campaign with working on it. Supply materials and spend time immediately creating publicity.

If your time does not allow immediate follow-up, e-mail or call tweens during the week to see how they are progressing with the preparations for the campaign.

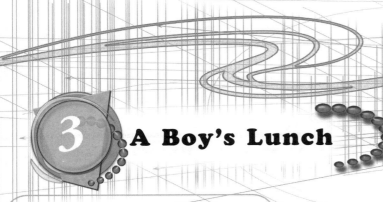

3 A Boy's Lunch

Supplies

- ❑ Bibles
- ❑ Banner-making supplies
- ❑ Tape or other fasteners to hold up the banner for display
- ❑ Folding card table
- ❑ Extra-small plastic bags for packaging baked goods (if needed)
- ❑ Water cooler and cups

LESSON IN A NUTSHELL

Missions need not always be about grand designs to make a difference. One of the greatest miracles that John recorded saw Jesus make use of the simple lunch that one boy was willing to share. The willingness to share when presented with a need can be a powerful experience for both the givers and the receivers.

DISCOVERING THE NEED

People who are traveling are often in a hurry, on a tight budget, and off their usual routines. Travelers are also often stressed. Any opportunities to share with them can brighten their day and create a ripple of goodwill—God's will.

Consider a local highway rest stop, bus or train station, harbor or airport as a place to set up a table in order to supply free drinks and food. Remember that the staff at these locations will be concerned about traffic flow and security, as well as competing with vendors in their vicinity. This activity will be best done in an area where all three of those concerns are the least, yet people still come through and wait for long periods.

GETTING READY

- ❑ A month before the event, contact your local bus or train station (or harbor or airport) to get approval to set up a table supplying free drinks and food. Even if you choose to use a park, contact the park department to obtain any necessary approval.
- ❑ A week before the event, remind the tweens and their parents to bring baked goods of some kind, preferably homemade. Ask that servings be packaged in small plastic bags.
- ❑ Prepare a large container of ice water, and make sure that you have plenty of cups available.
- ❑ Have a volunteer bake several cookies or other items specifically for the tweens when they return.
- ❑ Talk to a pastor about sharing Holy Communion at the closing.

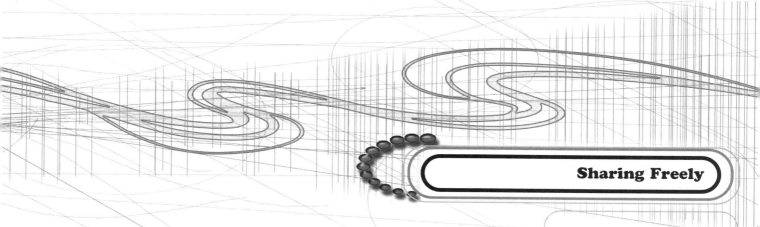

GATHER 'N' GAB (20–25 minutes)

As the tweens arrive, make a banner that identifies your group. Let the tweens decorate it, but remind them that this banner will form an early impression about them to anyone unfamiliar with the group. This banner may be reused for similar outings or made anew for each event.

Ask tweens to tell any interesting stories of their own travels.

Package any baked goods that need to be in serving-size bags.

GOD'S WORD (8–15 minutes)

Read aloud and have volunteers act out **John 6:1-14** (Feeding the 5,000).

The story of Jesus feeding several thousand people who came to hear him is throughout the Gospels. But John includes the story with a fundamental difference. The food isn't collected from several people; instead, a young boy actually provides the lunch Jesus blesses and multiplies. This story shows how necessary we are—even at a young age—to God's plans. The boy certainly didn't pack food for many people. But he was willing to share what he had when the disciples asked whether he had anything to contribute.

- How would you feel if some strangers came and asked you to share your lunch?
- Why do you think this story is in the Bible? What does it say to you?

TWEENS IN MISSION (60–90 minutes)

Roleplay approaching persons to offer the baked goods and water. What will the tweens say? What will they do? A few minutes of practice will be important. Gather everyone together and head to the station.

Find a good location that is accessible to many people yet doesn't disrupt the flow of people in the area (you will probably have already been assigned a place when you made arrangements to be there). If you have a contact person there, offer him or her some of the goodies as a thank you.

As people come by, offer them some baked goods. Make sure that the persons realize that you are not accepting donations but are merely sharing food with hungry travelers. If they insist on paying, you can suggest they make a donation to the chapel (if there is one on site) or another charity nearby.

Something to Consider

Create a special t-shirt for your tween group. Have the tweens wear their shirts to identify the group when they are on outings.

An alternative is to wear t-shirts that have the church name on them if you have such.

Remind the tweens not to stray from the group while they are at the station. Set up a buddy system also so that each person has someone else looking out for him or her.

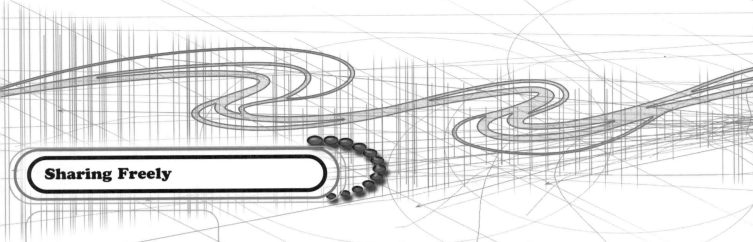

Sharing Freely

Notes

SNACK 'N' YACK (15–20 minutes)

It would be unfair to let the tweens be near all that food and not get any themselves, so serve refreshments and talk about the experience. Ask:

- How did people respond to your project?
- How did it feel to know that you helped some people?
- Did you feel God's presence at any point? When?

SENDING FORTH (2–20 minutes)

If you are sharing Communion, help the pastor set up the elements.

Whether or not you have Communion, remind the tweens that God can take little gifts and make great things happen from them. Close together in prayer.

Prayer: **We thank you, God, for meeting our needs. We have food to eat and places to stay and people who love us. Not everyone can say that, and so we pray for them. Look after those who are lacking basic needs. Help us see ways we can help even in our daily lives. We thank you for the opportunities you give us to share with others. We thank you for sharing with us. Amen.**

4 Special Day— Special Kids

LESSON IN A NUTSHELL

Your tweens will spend time with children who have physical, cognitive, emotional, and/or learning disabilities and will learn to see them as persons rather than just as persons with disabilities.

DISCOVERING THE NEED

Within most any community are children who live with disabilities. Some children are restricted to bed or wheelchairs or use orthopedic braces, walkers, or lifts. Some children are blind, deaf, or amputees; others have debilitating diseases or conditions, such as cerebral palsy, muscular dystrophy, spina bifida, or Down Syndrome. Often these children also live with loneliness. They may have few friends, if any, and may also experience a sense of being an "unseen person" as few people know how to relate to children with disabilities.

GETTING READY

❑ Begin by surveying your own congregation for special needs children. Consider helping them. Talk with their parents.

❑ Otherwise, consult your local phone book, a charitable funding agency, Special Olympics, or a hospital to discover which agencies and community ministries assist children with disabilities.

❑ Call one of them and speak to the director or volunteer coordinator to ask to schedule an activity with the children they serve.

❑ Choose games, activities, and food according to the director's suggestions. See whether board games, a sack lunch (or pizza) or a snack, and other activities are possible.

❑ Ask parents to help with supplying food and games from home.

❑ Find enough chaperones/drivers.

GATHER 'N' GAB (10–15 minutes)

As tweens arrive, prepare and pack all of the sack lunches or snacks. Make enough for your tweens, the chaperones, and the children you will visit. Talk about the place and the children you will be visiting. Ask the tweens about their experiences with persons with disabilities. Do they have friends, schoolmates, family members who have special needs?

Supplies

❑ Bibles

❑ Snack or supplies for sack lunches, including paper bags. Consider taking a sandwich, a bag of chips, an apple, and an individual drink for everyone. But be sure to check on suitability of the food.

❑ Board games and equipment for suitable group or outdoor games (Look also for non-competitive games. Do an Internet key word search for ideas.)

❑ Chaperones/drivers

❑ Large sheet of paper and markers

Special Tips

To interact well with children with disabilities:

- Focus on what the children do well, rather than on their disability.

- Avoid staring.

- Talk directly to the person; don't talk to someone else about the person when he or she can answer for himself or herself.

- Be flexible and helpful; this event is all about serving others.

- Use your friend-making skills. Assume that the child has something to bring to a friendship too. See him or her as a person.

- Relax and have a good time.

GOD'S WORD (20–25 minutes)

Say: **The story of Mephibosheth (mih-FIHB-oh-sheth) is one of the lesser known tales in the Old Testament. As a child, Mephibosheth suffered a tragic fall that left both his legs permanently crippled. With the death of his father and grandfather in battle, Mephibosheth would have lived in a ghetto-like home had it not been for the kindness of a man who took him into his own home.**

Years later, Mephibosheth received a letter inviting him to a state dinner. He was invited to be the guest of one of the leaders of his government.

To his amazement, this government official (King David) had been the best friend of his deceased father. And King David simply wanted to return ownership of the family land and to open his home in friendship.

The story of Mephibosheth and King David is one of honor and compassion, friendship and grace. It is a powerful illustration of God's love for us, and the kind of love God expects us to have for others.

Ask someone to read aloud **2 Samuel 9:1-13**. Ask:

- What difficulties do you think Mephibosheth faced in his day-to-day life because of his disability? What things would he likely not be able to do?
- How would most people have treated him?
- What would it feel like to lose your family home, property, and possessions?
- How do you imagine Mephibosheth felt when he entered the elegant surroundings of the banquet room and met this complete stranger?
- How would King David's kindness change Mephibosheth's life?
- Was King David trying to develop a long-term friendship, or was he simply returning property that didn't belong to him?
- What are some of the lessons of this story?

Make connections between the story and discussion of Mephibosheth, the experiences of the tweens have had with persons with disabilities, and the children your tweens will be visiting. Point out the need everyone has to be noticed and valued as a person, which is not always the case for children with disabilities.

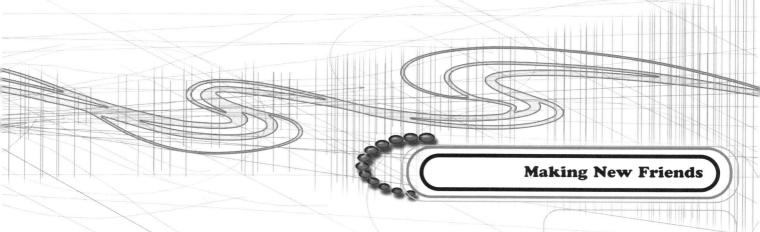

Ask the tweens about what is good to do and what is not good to do in relating to persons with disabilities. Make a list together. If the tweens do not come up with the points in Special Tips (page 70) on their own, be sure to bring them to their attention.

Pray together before leaving for the event.

TWEENS IN MISSION (90 minutes–2 hours)

Depending on the disability of the participants, any of the following activities might be considered:

- Board Game Olympics: To play several board games and establish a gold medal winner.

- Four Square Tournament, flag football, Frisbee® golf, and so forth.

- Other games or activities as recommended by the director of the facility

SNACK 'N' YACK (20–25 minutes)

Have the tweens serve the sack lunches and sit with a new friend. They could talk about such things as:

- Age, grade, school
- Favorite subject
- Favorite movie, book, color
- Hobbies
- What kind of pets they have
- And anything else that will help them develop a friendship

SENDING FORTH (2–3 minutes)

Gather together for a closing circle. Be sure that everyone is included. Pray with your new friends the following prayer from Numbers 6:24-26:

"The Lord bless you and keep you; the Lord make his face to shine upon you and be gracious to you; the Lord turn his face toward you and give you peace" (NIV).

Special Tips

On return trip in the car or back at the church take a few minutes to debrief the experience.

Ask the tweens:

- What did you enjoy?
- What surprised you?
- What did you learn from the experience?

5 A Servant's Attitude

Supplies

- ❑ Bibles
- ❑ Tools for the tasks (lawnmower, rakes, leaf bags, and so on)
- ❑ Garden gloves
- ❑ First-aid kit
- ❑ Permissions and emergency forms
- ❑ Magazines, scissors, paper, and glue
- ❑ Basin and towels

LESSON IN A NUTSHELL

We are very much a culture that desires to be served. This fact doesn't make us much different from the culture in which Jesus lived. But Jesus told us not to look down on those who serve, for he himself was but a servant. Your tweens will learn that service is something to be proud of and not embarrassed by.

DISCOVERING THE NEED

Most every church has members who are unable to leave their homes very often due to physical limitations. These persons who are homebound often find that they have neither the energy to take care of their homes the way they used to nor do they get many opportunities to visit with others. Your tweens can help a little bit with both of these needs.

GETTING READY

- ❑ Get a list of church members or neighbors who are homebound.
- ❑ Call them and request permission to come work on their yards. Tell them that the tween group is doing it simply out of love and not for fundraising. Let them know that the tweens would like to visit with them as well.
- ❑ Visit the sites in advance to determine the needed tasks.
- ❑ Gather lawnmowers, rakes, leaf bags, and other tools as necessary for taking care of the various yards. The persons you are helping may already have appropriate equipment at their houses; if so, ask whether you may use the equipment there. Be sure to check on its condition before the event.
- ❑ Make sure that you know how to properly dispose of any grass or trimmings, as per local ordinances and the homeowner's desires.
- ❑ Alert parents about the tasks their tweens will be doing; listen to and take into account any concerns they may have.
- ❑ Make sure that you have both a first-aid kit and medical emergency release forms.
- ❑ Have the tweens dress with appropriate shoes and long pants for safety.
- ❑ Provide magazines, scissors, paper, and glue.
- ❑ Bring a basin and towels for the closing.

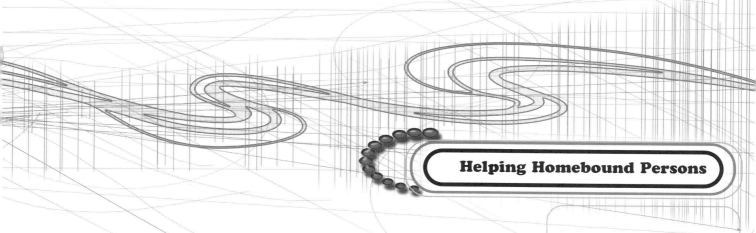

GATHER 'N' GAB (10–20 minutes)

As the tweens arrive, have several magazines scattered on a table. Ask the tweens to find and cut out pictures of people who are servants.

Share the results. Ask the tweens why they chose the pictures they did.

GOD'S WORD (15–25 minutes)

Read aloud **John 13:3-20** (washing of the feet). If there is time, use one or more of the activity options (see When Time Matters).

Say: **When Jesus and his disciples gathered for their final meal together, Jesus shocked them by insisting that he wash their feet. If you've ever worn sandals, you know how dirty your feet can get at the end of the day. If you wear sandals and spend most of your time outside and walk everywhere, your feet get even dirtier. If you live in a dusty area, it's even worse. In the days of Jesus, daily bathing was not a part of the culture. The disciples' feet were very dirty indeed!**

Ask:

- Why do you think Peter (and the other disciples) were so surprised that Jesus would wash their feet? (*Cleaning them was a task no one wanted to do and was certainly one Jesus would never be expected to do.*)
- Why do you think it was important to Jesus to wash the feet of his disciples? (*Jesus wanted to show them that God wanted them to serve others.*)
- How does the fact that Jesus chose to be a servant fit with the other things you know about Jesus?

Say: **There is nothing wrong with being served. Jesus allowed a woman to anoint him with oil (Matthew 26:6-13) and, in this very story, made the disciples accept being served. It is hard to serve others if they will not be served. But the point is that greatness comes from helping others, not by hoarding attention for ourselves.**

When Time Matters

If you have more time, have the tweens engage the foot washing story through any of these options:

- Act out the story.
- Pantomime the story as someone reads it .
- Draw a picture and talk about the depicted scene.
- Do a freeze-frame tabloid of Peter's shock. Then do one of the interaction after Jesus' explanation.

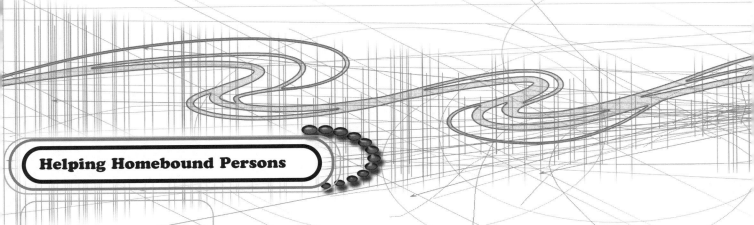

Helping Homebound Persons

Special Tips

It is possible that some of your tweens will have had little or no experience working in a yard or garden. Make safety a priority; teach the tweens safe practices. Coach individuals on the effective use of the tools for getting the job done. Encourage the young workers; acknowledge their efforts.

TWEENS IN MISSION (1–3 hours)

You may choose to go as a group to one home or to several. Or you may choose to divide the tweens into teams for each person on your list. Make sure that each team has at least one adult and any necessary tools.

Have the adults divide up the tasks, reminding the tweens that all tasks are important. These tasks include such things as mowing the grass, trimming hedges, raking leaves, weeding or clearing flower beds, and visiting with the homeowner. Assign different tasks at various points during the event, so that everyone does some manual labor and everyone has the opportunity to visit with the person the group is serving.

If you work with teams sent to different houses, have everyone return at the specified time.

SNACK 'N' YACK (20–25 minutes)

Set up a basin filled with fresh water. Place several towels nearby. Allow the youth the opportunity to clean up a bit after their work. Notice whether anyone offers to wash someone else's feet (and perhaps offer to do so yourself).

Serve refreshments and talk about the day's experiences. Ask:

- What surprised you the most about doing this project?
- Was your service well received? Did it go as you expected?
- Did you feel God's presence at any point? When?

SENDING FORTH (2–5 minutes)

Gather together around a focal point of a basin of clean water and a towel. (You may wish to set them on an altar.) You may also join in singing at least the chorus of "Jesu, Jesu." Close with prayer:

God, we confess that we would rather be served than serve. Let us find peace in service to others, knowing that we are doing as your very Son did during his ministry. Let us see service the way Jesus did, as a way to bring glory to you and blessings to both us and to those we serve. Amen.

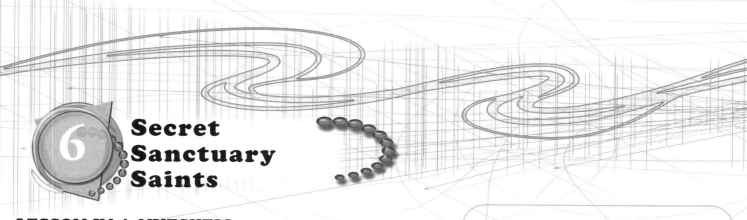

6 Secret Sanctuary Saints

LESSON IN A NUTSHELL

In this project, your tweens will have an opportunity to do something considerate for the church without seeking any praise or recognition.

DISCOVERING THE NEED

Tweens in worship probably never think about who cleans up the "pewage" of bulletins and children's drawings and other leftovers from worship. They may not even be aware that candles burn down over time and that someone is replacing them. These services are ones worshipers take for granted, but someone is serving the church in this way.

GETTING READY

❑ Contact the church office to determine who takes care of this. Make sure that the appropriate persons, including the custodial staff, are aware of your project. Coordinate this event with them.

❑ Contact your church altar guild, worship committee, or pastor to make them aware of your plans. Most likely, the altar guild, worship committee, or the church office will be able to provide the candles, pencils, and other supplies needed.

❑ If it becomes necessary to order supplies, you will want to work through your church office.

GATHER 'N' GAB (10–12 minutes)

Move from your usual meeting place to the sanctuary. Have the tweens help take the supplies to the sanctuary.

Then send the group on a four-minute "pewage" hunt. They are not to pick up the leftover bulletins or drawings at this point—just to notice them. Have them look also for pew Bibles or hymnals that are out of place.

Have them return to a designated place and sit in the pews. Ask:

- When you come to worship, is the sanctuary so littered?
- What impression would a visitor have of how we honor God if the only evidence were how the sanctuary looks right now?

Supplies

❑ Bibles
❑ Small pew pencils
❑ Pencil sharpener
❑ Large plastic trash bag(s)
❑ Brass cleaner, old soft towels/rags
❑ Soft, clean gloves for handling the brassware
❑ Replacement candles for the sanctuary or refill solution (if liquid candles are used)
❑ Envelopes, visitor/prayer cards, and other cards typically placed in your church pews

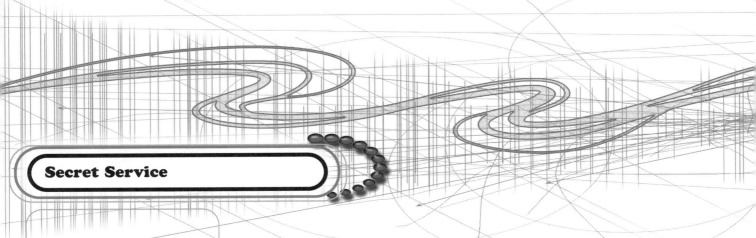

Secret Service

When Time Matters

If you have more time, you could expand the clean up to include washing and sanitizing the toys in the nursery.

Remind the tweens that young children put toys in their mouths. Cleaning the toys is not only a matter of making them look nicer but also of caring for the health of the children.

GOD'S WORD (10 minutes)

Have someone read aloud **Matthew 6:1-4.** Ask:

- What are some of the positive (honorable) reasons people do kind things? (*to be helpful, to follow the example of Jesus, to honor God*)
- What are some of the negative (self-serving) reasons people do kind things? (*to show off, to gain recognition or awards, to feel important, to receive praise and applause*)

Say: **Today's Bible passage gives us some insights about helping others. Being helpful is not about getting praise or recognition. It's not about showing off or impressing others. It's simply something Christians should do with love and humility.**

The Message version of the Bible says,

> **"When you help someone out, don't think about how it looks. Just do it—quietly and unobtrusively."**

In other words, do it without showing off or expecting anyone to pat you on the back. Therefore, as we serve as Secret Sanctuary Saints, don't expect any recognition in the newsletter or cards of appreciation. Today we're serving God without any fanfare or expectation of recognition.

In our secrecy, God will be honored and our church will be helped.

Pray: **Dear God, although others will be unaware of our kind act today, we know that you are aware and watching and cheering us on. May our act of secret service be a demonstration of our love for you. Amen.**

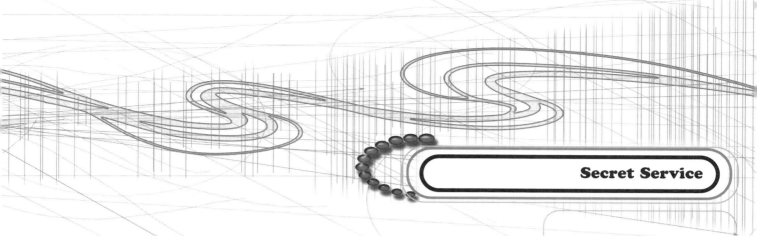

TWEENS IN MISSION (20–30 minutes)

Use the large trash bag to dispose of old bulletins and trash. Be sure to check inside hymnals and hymnal racks. Don't forget about the choir loft, balcony, alcoves, annex seating, and other places where old bulletins are discarded.

Straighten up or return Bibles and hymnals to the pew racks.

Use a good brass cleaner to shine the candle holders, brass cross, and other brass altar implements.

Sharpen or replace all of the short pencils in the pew racks.

Refill the envelope holders with the items typically found in your church pews. This may include, but is not limited to, prayer cards, visitor cards, offering envelopes, pledge cards.

Replace candles as needed. Some altar candles use a special refill solution. If this is true in your church, then you will need a bottle of the candle refill solution.

SNACK 'N' YACK (15–20 minutes)

While the tweens are finishing their snack, ask:

- Did you have fun?
- What did you enjoy doing most? least?
- How did it make you feel to help your church (and God)?
- How does it make you feel to serve in secret?
- Why did we (and the Bible) place an emphasis on secrecy today?

SENDING FORTH (2–3 minutes)

In your closing circle, ask the tweens to think of another opportunity for secret service that they, as individuals, can do. They may want to name those possibilities or simply think of them. Invite the tweens to follow through with that act of kindness.

Pray: **Dear God, help us serve you, regardless of the praise or recognition. Help us serve you because of our love for you. Amen.**

Special Tips

Be careful when using the brass cleaner. Read the directions and avoid direct contact with eyes. Use soft, clean gloves when handling the brassware.

Avoid the use of ink pens (instead of pew pencils). On hot summer days, ink pens tend to leak or explode, making a big mess on the pews, carpet, and clothing.

You might want to divide your group into teams, depending on the size of your sanctuary and/or the size of your group. An adult should supervise each group, particularly the ones working on the brass.

7 Portable Birthday Parties

Supplies

- ❑ Bibles
- ❑ Materials for making and decorating birthday cards and other party decorations
- ❑ Enough cupcakes for every person to be visited
- ❑ A box of birthday candles and matches or a lighter
- ❑ Birthday hats (and/or party favors) for everyone
- ❑ A small gift (example: homemade cookies) for every person visited; wrapping paper or gift bags
- ❑ Birthday card signed by the entire group. Homemade cards add a personal touch.
- ❑ Copies of the directions for your drivers
- ❑ One or two large blankets for the park (if needed)
- ❑ Food and drinks for the tweens

LESSON IN A NUTSHELL

In this event, your tweens will take the excitement of a portable birthday party to adults who are homebound, hospitalized, or institutionalized in your community.

DISCOVERING THE NEED

Celebrating a person's birthday is a good way to make him or her feel special—and everyone likes to feel special. Indeed, everyone is special in God's eyes. Persons who are homebound, hospitalized, or in a nursing home can easily lose sight of the joy of celebrating and feeling special. This surprise party can be a great pick up for persons whose lives have taken a downward turn.

Incidentally, choose people based on their need, not their actual date of birth. If they have a birthday anytime this year, they are eligible for this event. Although it may be July and their birthday is in November, they will still appreciate your visit.

GETTING READY

- ❑ Decide whether to visit in homes, nursing homes, or hospitals. Check with your pastor, staff, or senior adult ministries coordinator for guidance in determining whom to visit.
- ❑ You will also need to determine whether you will visit church members, non-members, or both. Also determine how many visits your group can handle in one afternoon.
- ❑ Coordinate nursing or hospital visits through their chaplain or volunteer coordinator. Coordinate homebound visits through your church office or staff. In each case, the staff associated with the persons you visit will help you determine when and where your help is most needed.
- ❑ Develop a list of names (or rooms to visit), along with directions to the facilities.
- ❑ Enlist enough drivers and chaperones.
- ❑ Distribute liability release and/or medical release forms.
- ❑ Have everyone bring a sack lunch; bring a few extra sandwiches for those who forget their sack lunch.
- ❑ Ask someone to provide a cooler of individual drinks.
- ❑ Make and decorate cupcakes.

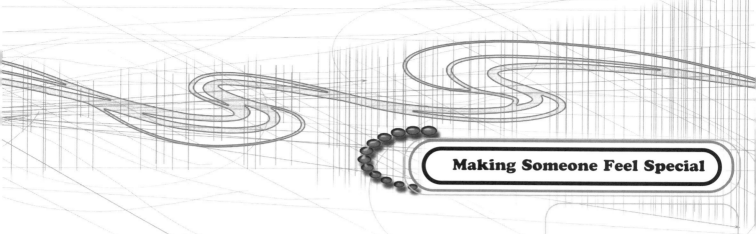

Making Someone Feel Special

GATHER 'N' GAB (10–20 minutes)

As the tweens arrive, invite them to make and decorate birthday cards, create decorations, and wrap the gifts.

Your tweens may arrive with questions and concerns about this event. Be sure to provide background information, to discuss the purpose of the project and the nature of the situation, and to address questions or concerns.

If visiting in a nursing home or hospital, prepare your tweens for the unusual sights and smells often associated with these facilities.

Be sure to discuss appropriate behavior. See Special Tips (page 80).

GOD'S WORD (8–10 minutes)

Have someone read aloud **Ezekiel 34:4-5** and **1 Thessalonians 5:11.**

Say: **In this first passage, Ezekiel was frustrated with the leaders of his day. He used the image of shepherds. Consumed by their own needs and concerns, they were neglecting the weak, sick, and injured. This passage is simply a warning never to forget those who depend on us.**

(So often, tweens consider themselves the leaders of tomorrow but not leaders of the church today. In this event, however, your tweens will lead the way in caring for the weak, sick, and injured.)

In the second passage, Paul reminds us to offer encouragement to one another.

Ask:

- Do you consider yourself a leader of the church? Why, or why not?
- Do you think that this Scripture applies to you? Explain.
- What will this project do for the weak, sick, and injured?
- How does this project bring encouragement? What lasting effects can this project have?
- How can this project strengthen our faith?

Pray: **Dear God, may our portable birthday parties bring encouragement and joy to the weak, sick, and injured in our community. May they sense our love and your presence. As we**

When Time Matters

If time is short, purchase birthday cards, decorations, and gift bags rather than have the tweens make them.

If you have more time, bring the cupcakes and decorating supplies and have the tweens frost and decorate them.

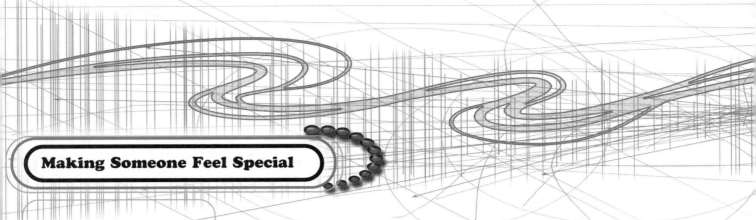

Making Someone Feel Special

Special Tips

To relate well to persons who are homebound, in the hospital, or in a nursing home:

- Stand or sit at an angle where the person can see you easily.
- If the person is bedridden, don't sit on the bed.
- Speak clearly so that the person can hear you easily.
- Focus on making the time special for the person.
- Listen respectfully when the person talks.
- Don't stare at, point at, or make fun of anyone.

depart, bless the persons we will visit, give us the words to say, and empower us with your Spirit. Amen.

TWEENS IN MISSION (60–90 MINUTES)

Load your supplies into the vehicles. Address last-minute questions.

Make your visits. Stay for 10–25 minutes, as deemed appropriate. Light the candle on the cupcake, sing "Happy Birthday," and present the honoree with a small birthday gift.

Spend some time getting to know your new friend. If needed, use the following discussion questions:

- Did you have any unusual birthday traditions when you were growing up?
- What was your most memorable birthday?
- Have you ever given or received a surprise birthday party? (If he or she has, ask: What was it like?)
- What was the best birthday gift you ever received?

SNACK 'N' YACK (25–30 minutes)

Go to a park to eat. While the tweens are finishing their meal, ask:

- Had you ever met this person (these persons) before? What did you learn about him or her (them)?
- Did he or she (they) seem to appreciate our visit?
- Did we stay too long or not long enough? How could you tell?
- How did the party (parties) make you feel?
- How do you suppose our visit made him or her (them) feel?
- Do you think our visit was (visits were) helpful? If yes, to whom?

SENDING FORTH (5–8 minutes)

Gather into a circle. Pass a lighted cupcake carefully from person to person. Whoever has the cupcake is to pray for or name someone who needs encouragement. The tween does not need to speak aloud; he or she may simply pass the cake. Close with this prayer:

Dear God, help us be good shepherds, to care for the weak, sick, and injured. Give us hearts of compassion and a commitment never to neglect those who are depending on our love. Help us build up others with encouragement; help us make others feel special. Amen.

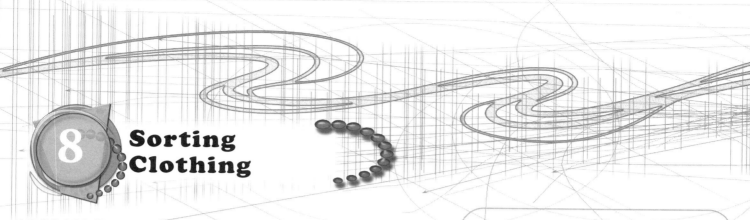

8 Sorting Clothing

LESSON IN A NUTSHELL

Your tweens will sort clothing (and perhaps assist with other minor projects) at a local clothes closet, night shelter, or community service organization. This service will ultimately benefit persons in need.

DISCOVERING THE NEED

Most tweens do not think twice about having clothes. But many individuals and families struggle financially or experience disasters, such as a house fire, making it difficult for them to get clean, serviceable, and even "nice" clothes. Agencies often receive donations but need volunteers to prepare clothes for distribution.

GETTING READY

❑ Contact your local Salvation Army, United Way, clothes closets, inner city ministries, and care-giving agencies to begin selecting a group to assist. Your pastor or mission committee chairperson may be able to point you in the right direction.
❑ Involve your tweens in choosing a place to serve.
❑ Contact the volunteer coordinator and schedule a date and time.
❑ Be sure to discuss mutual expectations, the time frame, age restrictions, and so on.
❑ Schedule your group for a tour and explanation of the ministry.
❑ Arrange for a quiet place for the group to eat there.
❑ Make a pre-trip visit by yourself. It is usually beneficial to visit the ministry site in advance. That way you can address questions and concerns with a reasonable degree of confidence and give the tweens a clearer idea of what to expect.
❑ Enlist chaperones and drivers for the event.
❑ Invite the tweens and other church members to donate clothing, which you can take with you. Publicize the request in a variety of ways (newsletter, posters, e-mail, direct mail, phone calls, bulletin).
❑ Distribute permissions forms.
❑ Ask one of the parents to prepare a to-go snack or lunch—something you can eat at the ministry site.
❑ Be flexible. When you arrive, the agency may have other projects for you to tackle (for example, cleaning, stacking boxes, moving items, and so on). Be sure to help however your help is needed.

Supplies

❑ Bibles
❑ Donated clothing items to take with you
❑ To-go snack or lunch
❑ Various clothing catalogs, including ones that have clothing for children
❑ Posterboard sheets and markers
❑ Glue and scissors

Clothing the 'Naked'

Special Tips

This is a fairly easy activity to organize, but you will need to plan to make sure things run smoothly. Most organizations typically need a few weeks notice.

Some agencies have minimum age requirements. Therefore, this is one of the first matters you will want them to address.

GATHER 'N' GAB

Talk to your tweens briefly about the schedule and nature of the project; give them some background information about the facility and its ministry. Ask:

- Do you know anyone who has lost everything in a fire or other disaster?
- What immediate needs would a family in that situation have?

Invite the tweens to form "family" groups. The imaginary families can be three to five persons. Have the tweens decide the adults, youth, and children that make up their family (for example, a single parent and two children, ages ten and seven; a mother and father, a thirteen year old, a nine year old, and an infant; a grandmother who is the guardian of her two five-year-old grandchildren, who are cousins).

Give each family group some clothing catalogs and have them "shop" for clothing for the family members. They need to select clothes for four to seven days (you decide, based on the time you have available for this activity). They may cut out the items and glue them to their posterboard for their family, but they must keep track of the cost of each item and of the total for the family members and for the family as a whole. Tell the tweens that they are not to go for really expensive items but to choose ones that are on the lower end of the pricing scale.

Gather the tweens; and together list what else, besides clothing, families have to pay for.

Then have the tweens present their families and their dollar totals. Ask:

- How is the work we will be doing today a ministry?

GOD'S WORD

Have volunteers read aloud **Matthew 25:34-40** as a dialogue. Have a narrator read the introductory phrases, verses 34a, 37a, and 40a. One person (the king) will read verses 34b-36 and 40b; the rest of the group (the righteous) will read verses 37b-39.

Say: **Sadly, poverty and disasters, which cause homelessness, hunger, and lack of clothing, are persistent problems. However, there are things we can do—although they may seem small——to make a difference. And today's activity is an example of that.**

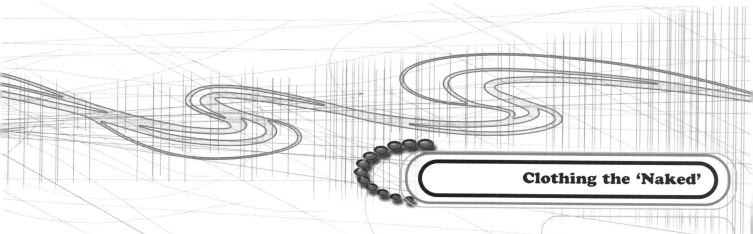

Unfortunately, some people look at the problem of poverty, especially, and become overwhelmed. Consequently, they do nothing out of frustration. Yet, the enormity of the problem shouldn't stop us from doing our part. Although we can't change the world, we can change a small portion. It's just a matter of caring and doing what we can, recognizing that as we serve God's people, we serve God.

TWEENS IN MISSION (60–90 minutes)

❑ Drive to the facility.
❑ Help sort clothing as directed.
❑ Assist with other projects as needed.
❑ Take a tour of the facility if possible.

SNACK 'N' YACK (20 minutes)

Ask the following questions as your group enjoys meal time:

- What did you enjoy most about today's project?
- What did you enjoy least?
- Did the volunteers (or staff) seem to appreciate our help?
- In what ways did we help the volunteers (or staff)?
- Are there other ways we can help them in the future?

SENDING FORTH (3–5 minutes)

If you are able, have each tween select an item of clothing to hold. Ask the tweens to pray silently for the person who will receive the clothing.

Pray: **Dear God, please bless the people who come to this agency (ministry) seeking help because of poverty or disaster. Bless this agency (ministry) in its efforts to provide persons with basic necessities, like clothing. May we be faithful in doing our part, however great or small, to to serve your people. Amen.**

Special Tips

Some organizations store old clothing in boxes, warehouses, closets, hallways, musty basements, or storage bins. Therefore, your work space may be cluttered, crowded, and even dark or musty. Don't let that surprise you. Be flexible and prepared to work in any environment.

Discourage your tweens from making fun of the clothing or facility, or trying on or destroying items.

9 Peace to This House

Supplies

- ❑ Bibles
- ❑ Helium tank
- ❑ Helium-quality balloons
- ❑ String or ribbon
- ❑ Plastic coat hanger
- ❑ Scissors

LESSON IN A NUTSHELL

We can forget exactly what the purpose of our mission work is. We don't engage in missions to recruit new members or feel good about ourselves. We do it to spread the love of God, as we are commanded to do. Your group will learn that spreading God's love is central to the life of mission and is the reward in and of itself.

DISCOVERING THE NEED

Sometimes people just need a word of encouragement, a word of hope, a word of peace. A local park, where people are going for recreation and relaxation, is a good place for such kindness. A supermarket entrance, where people go about their harried lives, may also be a good place.

GETTING READY

- ❑ Check with your local parks department or supermarket to make sure that this activity doesn't violate any ordinances or policies. Some places will also require permits for any distributions.
- ❑ Rent a helium tank. You will probably need to make arrangements for the rental at least a week ahead of time. Purchase several helium-quality balloons (at least 50, but you may want more if you think you will go through them quickly). You might want specially printed balloons with the name of your church on them, but remember that this mission isn't really about advertising.
- ❑ Also purchase plenty of string or ribbon.

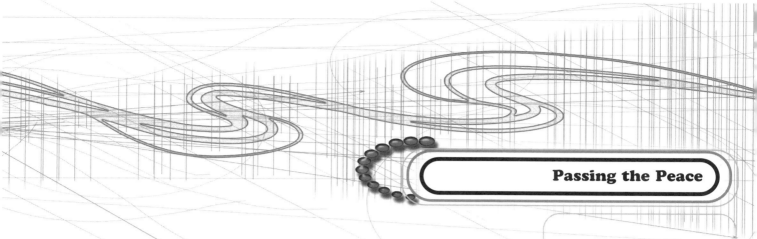

GATHER 'N' GAB (10 minutes)

As the tweens arrive, ask them to tell of their experiences of visiting the homes of strangers. Especially if any tweens have visited foreign cultures, have the tweens talk about what they were like.

GOD'S WORD (8–12 minutes)

Read **Luke 9:1-6** (Sending of the Twelve) and **Luke 10:1-9** (Sending of the Seventy). Reread **Luke 10:5-6**.

Luke tells two different accounts of Jesus sending his followers out during his ministry to spread his message and to heal people. When the seventy are sent out, Jesus tells them to say to those they visit, "Peace to this house!" If they are met in peace, those who dwell there experience God's peace. This word of peace begins their ministry among the people.

- What would it be like if someone were to come to your home and say, "Peace to this house"? How would you feel? What would you do?
- What would such peace look like to most people? What would it look like to you?

Say: **People have many needs, but everyone could use some of God's peace.**

TWEENS IN MISSION (45–90 minutes)

Gather the supplies and head to your local park. You may choose to inflate the balloons and then travel, or you may wait until you are on location to fill the balloons.

Have several people (including at least one adult) inflate and tie off balloons. Make sure that the balloons are all attached to something (a plastic coat hanger works well for this) so that they do not float away before you can give them away.

Have the tweens distribute the balloons to persons of all ages. (**Important: Ask parents before giving balloons to small children since latex balloons and the strings attached to them are a choking hazard for children under three years old.**) The tweens need to tell people they give the balloons to that there are "no strings attached," except the one physically on the balloon. Remind the tweens to say to recipients, "Peace be with you."

After the allotted time, return to your meeting place.

Special Tips

If you don't already have one, make a banner that identifies your group. Let the tweens decorate it, being sure to tell the tweens that this banner will form an early impression about them to anyone unfamiliar with the group. This banner can be reused for similar outings or made anew for each event.

You may already have t-shirts that identify your group (see the bottom of page 51). If so, these will likely be easier to manage than a banner.

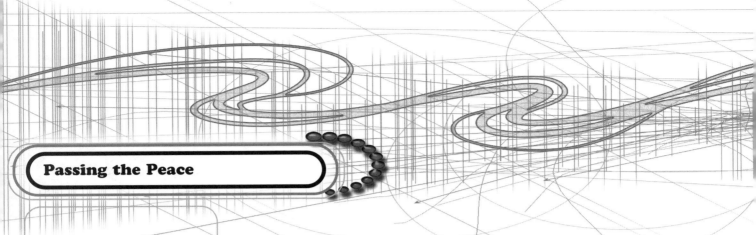

Passing the Peace

Special Tips

Employ a buddy system so that the tweens are in pairs as they hand out the balloons.

SNACK 'N' YACK (20 minutes)

Serve refreshments and talk about the experience. Ask:

- Did you get any strange questions or looks? How did you respond?
- Do you think the balloons brightened people's day?
- What do you think they will take home from your encounter (besides the balloon)? What will you take home?
- Did you feel God's presence at any point? When?

SENDING FORTH (7–10 minutes)

Ask the tweens to find a quiet spot within sight of the group and reflect on God's presence in their lives. After five minutes, pull everyone back together.

If your congregation has a tradition of passing the peace during worship, the tweens will be familiar with this ritual. If not, introduce it. Tell the group that as part of worship or Holy Communion, many churches do a "passing of the peace." It is simply a time of greeting one another in recognition of God's desire for peace for all of us. The traditional greeting is "The peace of Christ be with you." The traditional response is "And also with you." The exact words do not matter; it's the spirit of the greeting. The words may be accompanied by a handshake, a nod, or a hug.

Close in prayer:

God, sometimes we just need a break. Life can seem overwhelming and out of control. We need your peace to make it through our lives. We pray that not only may we find that peace, but that others may too. Whether they face actual violence or just don't know what to do with themselves, we pray that your Spirit will find them and comfort them. Let it also comfort us. In the name of Jesus, we pray, Amen.

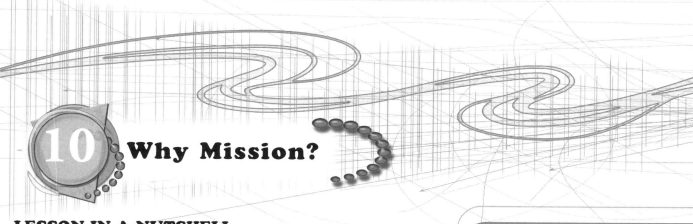

10 Why Mission?

LESSON IN A NUTSHELL

This lesson will explore what mission is, how it should be carried out, and why we do it. The tweens will prepare busy bags for children for use in the congregational worship services as an act of mission.

DISCOVERING THE NEED

Small children have a difficult time being still during worship. These children aren't meaning to be rude; they simply must engage more senses than just hearing words that are targeted for adults.

GETTING READY

❑ Talk with your pastor about the idea. He or she may also direct you to worship committee.
❑ Gather supplies for busy bags. If you are asking for donations of supplies, determine when and how you will do so.
❑ Gather supplies to decorate the bags themselves.

GATHER 'N' GAB (12–20 minutes)

As the tweens arrive, have the words "FAITH + WORKS = MISSION" written on a wipe-off board or posterboard. Ask the tweens to work together in pairs or small groups to come up with as many words with four or more letters as they can make from the words.

Once everyone has arrived, ask the tweens to then write as many different terms they can think of relating to the word *mission*.

GOD'S WORD (12–25 minutes)

Have everyone read **James 2:14-17.** Have the tweens work in small groups to come up with skits that illustrate the Scripture. The tweens may use the ideas in verses 15–16 as a starting point, but challenge them to think of other situations as well. They may do a skit to illustrate the negative (faith without works) or the positive (faith with works).

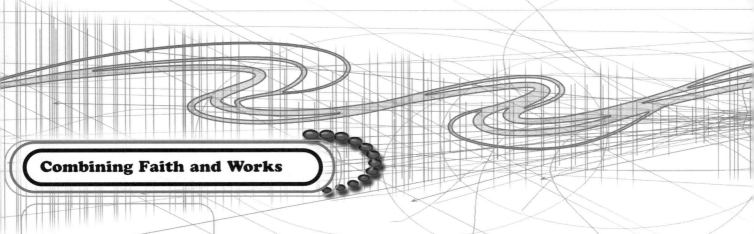

Combining Faith and Works

Notes

As an alternative to skits, have the tweens draw pictures of situations that illustrate either the negative or the positive. Be sure to have the tweens talk about what they chose to illustrate.

Ask:

- Why do we do mission work?

Say: **We have an important job to do: telling people the good news of Jesus Christ. We can't just do that with our words; we need to "speak" with our actions as well. God wants us to treat everyone as a child of God, because all people matter to God. When we don't help others, we move away from God. Here's a way to think about that.**

Have the tweens gather into a circle and stand shoulder to shoulder. Tell them to pretend that God is in the center of their circle. Then have them take two or three big steps away from the center. Ask:

- When we move away from our center, God, what else changes? (*We move farther away from one another.*)

Then have the tweens move as close to one another as possible. Ask:

- When we come together, what else changes? (*We move closer to God.*)

TWEENS IN MISSION (20–30 minutes)

Have the tweens decorate paper bags with glued items, paint, or markers. Tell the tweens that these bags will be used by small children and will be in the sanctuary of their church, so they need to be decorated appropriately. Suggest that the tweens use symbols, such as crosses, fish, wheat, grapes, rainbows, butterflies, and so on.

As the bags are drying, have the tweens sort out the supplies for each bag and then fill the bags.

Once the bags are ready, take them to the sanctuary for a blessing. Have the tweens call out the names of the small children they know who attend worship. If you have a list of other names, read it aloud too. Have the tweens pray together:

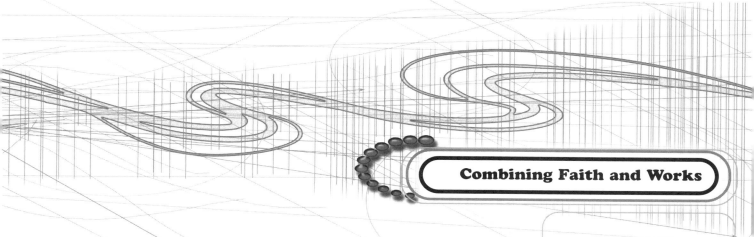

Dear God, we ask your blessing upon each of the children we have named and upon those whom we do not yet know who will come to worship in our church. We ask also that they will find our gift of these bags one that gives them joy. Amen.

Then the tweens may place the bags where they will be kept (either at the entrances or in the pews).

Have a tween write an article about the busy bags for the newsletter, explaining their purpose and thanking those who donated supplies.

SNACK 'N' YACK (10–15 minutes)

Serve refreshments and talk about the experience. Ask:

- Do you think that parents and their children will appreciate your work?
- Did you feel God's presence at any point? When?
- What are other ways you can act for God?

SENDING FORTH (2–5 minutes)

Ask the tweens to tell what worship means to them. Ask:

- Can mission work be a form of worship? Why, or why not?

Close in prayer:

Help us, God, to grow deeper in our knowledge of you through acting as you would have us act. Show us ways we can be of service to you and help your children wherever they may be. Grant us your Spirit so that we may meet the needs of others as well as our own needs. Let us be good servants of you. Amen.

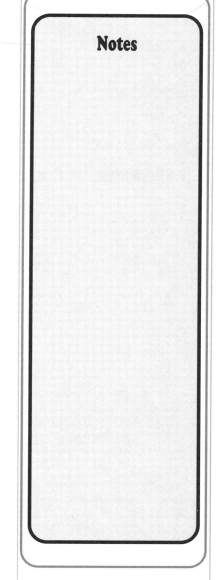

Notes

11 Book Binge

Supplies

- ❑ Bibles
- ❑ Books to donate
- ❑ Any equipment needed for chosen interactions, such as puppets or games (see page 92)
- ❑ Food and drinks for snack or a meal with the children

Something to Consider

Decide **what** books to collect:
- New books, used books, or both?
- Books written for preschoolers, children, and/or teenagers?
- Christian books only or simply books that convey good values?

Decide **how** to collect the books:
- Using collection receptacles?
- Bringing books to the altar during a special worship service?
- Dropping them off at the church office or satellite location?
- Allowing people to donate money but purchasing the books yourself?
- Using an "Adopt-a-Book" format— purchasing the books in advance and simply asking people to adopt-a-book from your book display (by paying the price on a posted receipt)?

If you purchase the books, take advantage of sales and discounts. Ask the bookstore manager for a discount on a large purchase. Some Internet bookstores offer discount prices and free shipping with a minimum purchase.

LESSON IN A NUTSHELL

Your tweens will collect and deliver quality books to a local children's home, daycare, or community facility for children. More importantly, they will spend time with the children, following Jesus' example of welcoming the children to be with him.

DISCOVERING THE NEED

Books open the world to children. The stories and pictures speak to their souls and allow imagination to take flight. For children, reading with someone is an opportunity for cuddling and feeling special, for exploring new ideas and gaining knowledge, for growing in the crucial skill of reading.

Organizations are often in need of high-quality children's books. Here's an example of the types of organizations you could help:

> Head Start, an inner-city preschool, children's home, daycare center, community center, children's hospital, pediatric wing of a hospital, hospital waiting rooms

GETTING READY

- ❑ Choose an organization with values and a mission similar to the values and mission of your church.
- ❑ Set up the project through the organization's volunteer coordinator. Work with him or her to develop a list of books (or the types of books) to be collected.
- ❑ Will the organization allow interaction with their children? If yes, work with their volunteer coordinator to develop ways for your tweens to interact with their children. For instance, reading with them, playing some games, performing a skit or play of one of the books, or having a story time. (See the list on page 92 also.)
- ❑ If interaction with the children is not possible, then schedule a time when your tweens can deliver the books.
- ❑ Arrange for a tour of the facility, if possible.
- ❑ Review the considerations listed in the margins on pages 90–92 before determining what you will solicit from the congregation.
- ❑ Publicize the project and the books needed.
- ❑ Distribute medical/liability release forms.

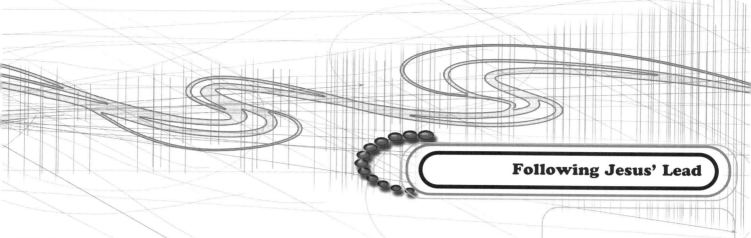

❑ Enlist chaperons and drivers to help. One of your vehicles may need to be a truck, SUV, or van (for the books).

❑ Determine how you will move the books—crates, boxes, sturdy bags. Take enough containers to deliver the books.

❑ Provide snacks or a light meal for everyone. Parents may be enlisted to help with this. If not, each tween may be asked to bring a large bag of chips or a two-liter drink.

GATHER 'N' GAB (10–15 minutes)

Invite the tweens to look through the books for a few minutes. Then have them help package them in boxes or bags and load them into the vehicles to take to the children.

Meet briefly with your tweens to discuss the agenda and purposes of the event, and to address any of their questions or concerns. Be sure to supply background information about the agency, and collect the permission forms.

GOD'S WORD (10 minutes)

Have someone read aloud **Matthew 19:13-14.**

Say: **Although the disciples considered the little children an intrusion or annoyance, Jesus welcomed and even encouraged their presence. Blessing the children was not beneath the dignity of this Messiah. He was forever paying attention to those whom the world would push aside.**

Ask:

- What does it mean to "bless" or "be a blessing" to others? (*To be blessed is to be granted special favor by God. Joy, quite frequently, is the human response to God's blessings.*)
- Today we have an opportunity to bless God's little children. In what ways can our actions and gifts be a blessing to others? If Jesus were here, what might he say about our gifts?

Say: **As followers of Christ, we have the responsibility of being a blessing to others too. Today's project gives us such an opportunity.**

Pray: **Dear God, use these gifts to bless those whose lives are in need of your joy. Guide our steps and use our faithfulness to bless others. Amen.**

Considerations

You may want to invite local bookstores to donate books, sell books at a reduced price, or set up a display in your foyer or fellowship hall for purchases by the congregation.

Think about the timing of this project. Would it fit your congregation's plans for Christmas time or some other holiday? What about making it part of your annual stewardship, mission emphasis, or Children's Sabbath?

91

Following Jesus' Lead

Special Tips

- Give clear instructions when asking for donations of children's books. Otherwise, you may receive everything from out-of-date textbooks to coloring books.

- Encourage people to purchase books in memory or honor of someone.

- Have a dedication ceremony for the books and their recipients in your congregational worship service.

- Write the questions in Snack 'n' Yack on index cards and give them to your tweens to prompt their conversations with the children if necessary.

TWEENS IN MISSION (1–2 hours)

Deliver your books to your chosen organization. Tour the facility.

Spend time with the children. Use these ideas for interaction:

❏ Play non-competitive games. Search this topic on the Internet; and you will discover a variety of games that emphasize fellowship and interaction, rather than winners and losers.
❏ Use team-building games. These promote a sense of camaraderie and unity.
❏ Read one-on-one with the children. Have your tweens pair off with a child and read a book together. The tween and child can take turns reading.
❏ Perform a skit or puppet show based on one of the books you are delivering.
❏ Play together. If the organization has a playground, your group may interact with the children on the playground.
❏ Have story time. One of your tweens (or adults) may serve as a storyteller, reading one of the more popular and interesting books to the group.
❏ Host a snack or meal time with the children.

SNACK 'N' YACK (20–30 minutes)

Spend time enjoying snacks or a light meal with your new friends. Your tweens might like to use some of these questions:

- What is your favorite book?
- Who is your favorite storybook character? Why?
- If you could write a book, what would it be about? Why?
- Would you like to help me draw a picture of your favorite storybook character(s)?

SENDING FORTH (5–7 minutes)

Ask the tweens where they saw God today or where they saw or received a blessing themselves from this day's project. Close with prayer:

Dear Jesus, help us follow your example and never look upon little children as a nuisance or intrusion, but rather precious souls who are worthy our time, attention, and concern. Amen.

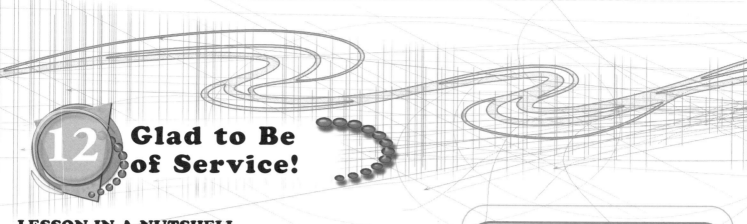

12 Glad to Be of Service!

LESSON IN A NUTSHELL

Many people do so much good work that seemingly isn't noticed. But God notices! Your group will identify and thank some of those who help others; they will also participate in work of their own without expecting thanks.

DISCOVERING THE NEED

When children are in strange situations, they need comforting. Time in a hospital is especially difficult. In addition to being ill or injured, children feel cut off from family, friends, and their routine. A reminder of God's presence is a welcome gift.

You may need to choose between multiple hospitals to visit. Ideally, a hospital that is part of your congregation's community is best. If there is a children's hospital, that is an obvious possibility; check to see if other hospitals also have children, as these children can often be forgotten.

GETTING READY

❑ Contact a nearby hospital and find out whether outside groups are allowed to bring stuffed animals to children who are patients. Ask whether your group will be allowed to give snacks to staff, as well.

❑ Publicize the mission well in advance, asking the congregation to donate new stuffed animals to be given to children in the hospital.

❑ A week before the visit, call the department or departments you will be visiting to remind them that your group is coming.

❑ A day before the visit, call the departments again and request an approximate total. Make sure that you have enough for every child in the unit you visit, plus four or more extras. The number of patients in a hospital unit can vary dramatically from day to day, so keep that in mind.

❑ Have on hand paper and ribbons to attach notes to each animal.

❑ Bake cookies or brownies or make candy to fill one or more snack plates to be delivered to the nurses' station.

Supplies

❑ Bibles
❑ Donated new stuffed animals
❑ Snack plate for nurses' station (cookies, brownies, candy, paper plate, wrap, and ribbon)
❑ Paper for making note cards
❑ Markers or paints
❑ Pens or pencils
❑ Ribbon
❑ Scissors
❑ Paper punch
❑ Snack for the tweens
❑ Rhythm instruments

Reminders of God's Presence

When Time Matters

If you have more time, have the tweens help make the cookies or brownies. Bake the treats while you prepare the stuffed animals and do the Bible study.

GATHER 'N' GAB (10–15 minutes)

As the tweens arrive, prepare the snack plate(s) for the staff and write a thank-you note. Also divide the animals among the tweens and have them write notes to attach to the animals. Tell the tweens that the note should read,

> "We have said a prayer for you with your new friend. This friend is a small reminder that you are loved and that God is always with you."

The tweens may decorate the notes. You may want them to write the church's name on it. Have them punch a hole in the note card and use the ribbon to tie it to the stuffed animal.

GOD'S WORD (12–20 minutes)

Have the tweens open their Bibles and together read Psalm 117. Then have some fun by putting rhythm and movement to verse 2. If you have a small group, they can work together to create a rhythm for the verse, using rhythm instruments, table tops, or body parts to set the rhythm. If you have a large group, divide them into smaller groups and let each group devise its own rhythm. Bring the groups back together and let each small group take turns performing its version of verse 2 to the entire group.

After your music interlude, have the tweens break into three groups. Assign each group one of the following words from Psalm 117:2: Group 1: *steadfast*, Group 2: *faithfulness*, and Group 3: *forever*. Ask each group to talk about what these words mean and to come up with their own definition of their word and one example of how they think of God as being like the word they were assigned. As the leaders, you and other adults should move from group to group. However, allow your tweens to do most of the struggling with the concepts.

After sufficient time, have each group tell what its word means and how they think God is like that word.

TWEENS IN MISSION (40–60 minutes)

Gather the stuffed animals into the sanctuary and pray over them.

Prayer: Loving and compassionate God, we pray that you will bless these gifts and those children who will receive them. We ask that the children will feel your presence and your love. May these gifts bring comfort and hope to the children who hold them or who are near them; may they always know that

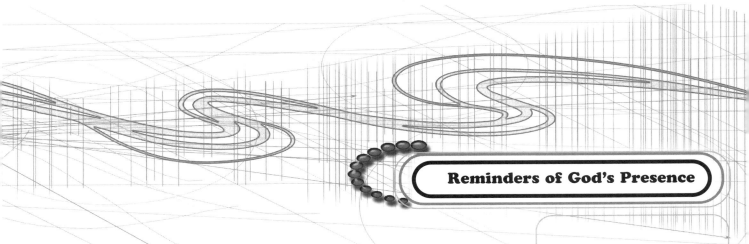

they are loved. Bless also those who care for the children; may they bring healing and compassion to their patients. We ask also that your Spirit will be with us as we deliver these gifts, so that all who see us will truly see you at work. In the name of our Savior Jesus Christ we pray. Amen.

Collect all the animals and the gifts for the staff. Go to the hospital. Remind the tweens that they have to be more careful than normal and that they must follow the rules closely or they won't be allowed to share their gifts.

Distribute the animals to the children in the unit you contacted. If you brought a snack for the staff, make sure they receive that as well.

Encourage the tweens to talk to the children as they distribute the animals. The children, especially older ones, will appreciate any visiting.

SNACK 'N' YACK (15–20 minutes)

Serve refreshments and talk about the experience. Ask:

- How did the children or their parents react to your gift? How about the staff?
- What surprised you about your visit?
- Did you feel God's presence at any point? When?
- How could you continue this project?

SENDING FORTH (2–3 minutes)

Gather together for prayer. Remind the tweens of **Psalm 139:** God knows us each intimately—even before we were born; God is with us no matter where we are (including a hospital); God will be with each of us at our end. God loves us.

Prayer: God, we are so grateful that neither we nor these children must face difficult times alone. Thank you for the gift of your love for us and for your constant presence. We pray for each of these children, for their families, and for the staff who are instruments of your healing. We pray that each time the children see one of our stuffed animals, they will be comforted and feel loved. Amen.

Special Tips

Have the tweens wash their hands before handling the stuffed animals or food and before leaving for the hospital. Most of your group will know that hand washing is a key way to avoid the spread of germs.

Be aware that seeing children of their own age or younger who are ill or injured may be disturbing to your tweens. Some may ask about children dying. Be honest: you do not know if the child will die; you do know that God is present in life and in death.

Books Especially for Leaders of Tweens

Tween Time: Fellowship and Service Projects for Preteens (Volume 1). 12 Fellowship programs and 12 service projects based on Scripture, plus essential leader information about this unique age level. For grades 5–6. ISBN: 0687022541.

Tween Spirituality: Offering Opportunities in Preteen Spiritual Growth. A book for teachers with articles on tweens' spirituality and specific activities to nourish spiritual habits. Reproducible section for use with parents. ISBN: 0687075513.

Holy Happenings, by Andy Robb. Six books packed with facts, jokes, cartoons, and thought-provoking questions cover all of the major themes of the Bible. Tweens will be encouraged to open their Bibles to learn more about the characters they meet.

Ballistic Beginnings
ISBN: 068702336X
Hodgepodge Hebrews
ISBN: 0687023262
Magnificent Moses
ISBN: 0687023165
Catastrophic Kings
ISBN: 0687023068
Super Son
ISBN: 0687022967
Hyper Holy Happenings
ISBN: 068702286X.

Signs of Faith, by Marcia Stoner. This collection of Bible verses helps preteens and youth learn American Sign Language while performing an act of service for the church. ISBN: 0687099227.

BeTween Everything: Teacher Helps for Transitioning Tweens, by Ed Trimmer and Patty Myers. Helps teachers smooth the transition for preteens as they take the giant stops from childhood to adulthood. Provides a foundation for church ministry to ages 10–14. ISBN: 0687058287.

Symbols of Faith, by Marcia Stoner. More than 60 Christian symbols, with activities designed to teach each symbol. Reproducible patterns included for most symbols. ISBN: 0687094755.

Bad Stuff in the News, by Rabbi Marc Gellman and Monsignor Thomas Hartman. In this essential handbook, Gellman and Hartman, a.k.a. "The God Squad," help children and parents deal with confusing, troubling, and scary events while showing them how to take part in repairing the broken world around them.

Paperback—ISBN:1587172321.

Hardcover—ISBN: 1587171325.

Leader's Guide—ISBN: 0687075580.

Seasons of Faith, by Marcia Stoner. Offers activities based on the seasons of the Christian Year. Includes reproducible patterns and charts, an Advent worship booklet for use at church or at home, a Lenten study, Easter activities, and activities for Pentecost and World Communion Sunday. Includes a brief explanation of the history of each season. ISBN: 0687037360.